Joe Gould's Teeth

Joe Gould's Teeth

JILL LEPORE

 ALFRED A. KNOPF · NEW YORK · 2016

THIS IS A BORZOI BOOK
PUBLISHED BY ALFRED A. KNOPF

Copyright © 2015, 2016 by Jill Lepore

A version of this story appeared in *The New Yorker* in 2015.

Library of Congress Cataloging-in-Publication Data
Names: Lepore, Jill, [date] author.
Title: Joe Gould's teeth / by Jill Lepore.
Description: First edition. | New York : Alfred A. Knopf, 2016. |
"This is a Borzoi Book."
Identifiers: LCCN 2015035728 |
ISBN 9781101947586 (hardcover : alk. paper) |
ISBN 9781101947593 (ebook)
Subjects: LCSH: Gould, Joe, 1889–1957. | Oral history. |
Savage, Augusta, 1892–1962. | Biography—Methodology. |
New York (N.Y.)—Biography.
Classification: LCC CT9991.G6 L47 2016 |
DDC 974.7/1092—dc23
LC record available at http://lccn.loc.gov/2015035728

Front-of-jacket image: The National Archives,
London, England/Mary Evans
Jacket design by Kelly Blair

Manufactured in the United States of America
First Edition

To AA,
with love

The history of a nation is not in
    parliaments and battle-fields,
but in what people say to each other
on fair-days and high days,
and in how they farm, and quarrel,
and go on pilgrimage.

—W. B. YEATS

What am I always listening for in Harlem?

—ELIZABETH ALEXANDER

Contents

Meo Tempore

1

little joe gould has lost his teeth and doesn't know
   where
to find them

—E. E. CUMMINGS

For a long time, Joe Gould thought he was
going blind.[1] This was before he lost his teeth
and years before he lost the history of the world
he'd been writing in hundreds of dime-store composition notebooks, their black covers mottled
like the pelt of a speckled goat, their white pages
lined with thin blue veins.[2]

"I have created a vital new literary form," he
announced.[3] "Unfortunately, my manuscript is
not typed."[4]

He'd sit and he'd write and then he'd wrap his
black-and-white notebooks in brown paper, tie
them with twine, tuck them under one arm, and

tramp through the streets of New York, from Greenwich Village to Harlem. When he stopped, he'd untie his bundle, open a notebook, take out a pen, and begin again. He wore sneakers, a coat that didn't fit, owl's-eye glasses, and somebody else's teeth. He was writing the longest book ever written. He smoked and he drank and he listened. He said he was writing down nearly everything anyone ever said to him, especially in Harlem. He wrote until his eyes grew tired. He'd take his glasses off and forget where he'd set them down. How he lost his teeth is another story.

He began before the start of the First World War and didn't stop until after the end of the Second. He never finished. He called what he was writing "The Oral History of Our Time." (The title, with its ocular O's, looks very like a pair of spectacles.) In 1928, he told the poet Marianne Moore, who was editing a chapter of it for *The Dial*, that he'd come up with a better title.[5] "MEO TEMPORE seems to me intrinsically a good title," Moore wrote back, "but not better than the one we have."[6]

Joseph Ferdinand Gould is how he signed his name when he was feeling particularly grand, and when he was feeling even grander, he introduced himself as the most important historian of the twentieth century. "I believe you would be interested in my work," he wrote to George Sarton, the Harvard historian, in 1931. "I have been writing a history of my own time from oral sources. I use only material from my own experience and observation and from the direct personal narratives of others. In short, I am trying to record these complex times with the technique of a Herodotus or Froissart." Herodotus wrote his *Histories* in ancient Greece; Jean Froissart wrote his *Chronicles* in medieval Europe. Gould was writing his history, a talking history, in modern America.

"My book is very voluminous," he explained to Sarton:

> Apart from literary merit it will have future value as a storehouse of information. I imagine that the most valuable sections will be those which deal with groups that are inarticulate such as the Negro, the reservation Indian and the immigrant. It seems to me that the average person is just as much history as the ruler or celebrity as he illustrates the social forces of heredity and environment. Therefore I am trying to present lyrical episodes of everyday life. I would like to widen the sphere of history as Walt Whitman did that of poetry.[7]

For a time, he was rather remarkably well known. Chapters of his work appeared in avant-garde magazines nose to nose with essays by Virginia Woolf and drawings by Pablo Picasso. He went to parties with Langston Hughes. He dined with E. E. Cummings. He drank with John Dos Passos. He was sketched by Joseph Stella, photographed by Aaron Siskind, and painted by Alice Neel. Gould was a modernist, a lover of the vernacular, and a fetishist of form. He was ragged and, then again, he was fussy. "The Oral History of Our Time" was plainspoken, arresting, experimental, and disordered. Most notably, it was unremitting. So was he. Neel, when she painted him, gave him three penises.

Writers loved to write about him, the writer who could not stop writing. "The history is the work of some fifteen years of writing in subway trains, on 'El' platforms, in Bowery flop houses," the poet Horace Gregory wrote in *The New Republic*. "On Staten Island ferry boats, in smoking cars. In cheap and dingily exotic Greenwich Village restaurants, in public urinals."[8] And in Harlem, in crowded apartments, in smoky artists' studios, in public libraries.

"I am trying to be the Boswell and Pepys of a whole epoch," Gould liked to say.[9] He was Jacob Riis; he was John Lomax.[10] "I try to get the forgotten man into history," he told a reporter for the *New York Herald Tribune*.[11] If he was Herodotus, he was also Sisyphus. He wanted to jot down each jibber and every jabber. He started before broadcasting began, but once it did, its ceaselessness made his work harder. "The radio is beginning to cramp my style," he said.[12] It was rumored (though Gould himself disputed this) that he once smashed a radio to bits.

Naturally, writing down everything he heard took up nearly all his time. Sometimes, he made a living writing book reviews. At the height of the Depression he worked for the Federal Writers' Project; then he was fired.[13] He began to starve. He was covered with scabs and infected with fleas. "Met Joe il y a quesques jours &, b jeezuz, never have I beheld a corpse walking," Cummings wrote to Ezra Pound. Gould went on the dole. He lost his teeth, fakes. Cummings told Pound, "My sister says that if Joe can only keep on relief for a few years he'll have a new set of somebody's teeth."[14]

And what about the great work? In 1939, Dwight Macdonald, an editor of the *Partisan Review*, addressed the question of storage: "He has in 25 years managed to fill incalculable notebooks which in turn fill incalculable boxes."[15] He kept them in numberless closets and countless attics. "The stack of manuscripts comprising the *Oral History* has passed 7 feet," a reporter announced in 1941. "Gould is 5 feet 4."[16] His friends wished to have that stack published. "I want to read Joe Gould's Oral History," the short-story writer William Saroyan declared:

Harcourt, Brace; Random House; Scribner's; Viking; Houghton, Mifflin; Macmillan;

Doubleday, Doran; Farrar and Rinehart; all of you—for the love of Mike, are you publishers, or not? If you are, print Joe Gould's Oral History. Long, dirty, edited, unedited, *any* how—print it, that's all.[17]

But no one ever did. And no one knew, really, quite where it was.

"The Oral History is a great hodgepodge and kitchen midden of hearsay," Joseph Mitchell reported in *The New Yorker* in December 1942:

At least half of it is made up of conversations taken down verbatim or summarized; hence the title. "What people say is history," Gould says. "What we used to think was history—kings and queens, treaties, inventions, big battles, beheadings, Caesar, Napoleon, Pontius Pilate, Columbus, William Jennings Bryan—is only formal history and largely false. I'll put it down the informal history of the shirt-sleeved multitude—what they had to say about their jobs, love affairs, vittles, sprees, scrapes, and sorrows—or I'll perish in the attempt."[18]

Mitchell's profile of Gould is titled "Professor Sea Gull." It made Gould famous the world over.

"Professor Sea Gull" is one of the most influential literary essays ever published. People read it again and again. "I tasted every word," one far-away reader wrote to Mitchell.[19] The story was picked up by *Time* and reprinted here, there, everywhere. A U.S. Armed Services Edition was shipped to soldiers at the front. They tugged it out of their rucksacks and found they could not put it down. "Do you know how long it's been since we've had a piece that one couldn't stop reading?" a *New Yorker* editor asked Mitchell. "Since your last piece, that's how long."[20]

Calvin Trillin once compared Joseph Mitchell to Joe DiMaggio.[21] It stole your breath just to watch the man carry a bat. Mitchell didn't invent the *New Yorker* profile as a form, but he perfected it, precise, tender, and sly, with God-given prose.[22] Half Charles Dickens, half James Joyce, Mitchell loved to prowl the quirkier corners of New York, eavesdropping on eccentrics: Gypsies, hawkers, tightrope walkers. When Mitchell met Gould, it was as if he were looking at himself in a funhouse mirror. He saw, staring back at him, a clown:

> He dresses in the castoff clothes of his friends. His overcoat, suit, shirt, and even his shoes are all invariably a size or two too large, but he wears them with a kind of forlorn rakishness. "Just look at me," he says. "The only

thing that fits is the necktie." On bitter winter days he puts a layer of newspapers between his shirt and undershirt. "I'm snobbish," he says. "I only use the *Times*."

Mitchell's Gould was a natural democrat, the people's historian. He was also a bang-up reporter as uncanny as a tape recorder. "Gould puts into the Oral History only things he has seen or heard." It was as if Mitchell were describing his own notebook, a reporter's notebook, the notebook in which Mitchell, too, was forever writing down what people say. "He estimates that the manuscript contains 9,000,000 words," Mitchell wrote. "It may well be the longest unpublished work in existence."[23]

And maybe it was. But—and here's the trouble—Mitchell hadn't read more than a few pages of it. Instead, he'd mainly listened to Gould talk, jotting down each jibber and every jabber. Gould had little use for readers. "My impulse to express life in terms of my own observation and reflection is so strong," Gould once explained, "that I would continue to write, if I were the sole survivor of the human race, and believed that my material would be seen by no other eyes than mine."[24] For his eyes, alone, is, more or less, how it turned out.

. . .

Is a book a book if it has no readers? It's not as though no one had read "The Oral History of Our Time," but it would be fair to say that hardly anyone had read much of it and certainly no one had read all of it. "Mr. Ezra Pound and I once saw a fragment of it running to perhaps 40,000 words," Edward J. O'Brien, the editor of *Best Short Stories*, testified; he believed it had "considerable psychological and historical importance." Still, it was a mess. Pound put it delicately: "Mr. Joe Gould's prose style is uneven." Gould had an answer for that: "My history is uneven," he admitted. "It should be. It is an encyclopedia."[25]

It was, in any case, missing. Nearly everything Gould ever held in his hands slipped away. He lost his glasses; he lost his teeth. "I keep losing fountain pens, change, and even manuscripts," he wrote to William Carlos Williams. "I lost my diary in the toilet," he one day reported. "Bespectacled apologies!!!" he wrote Cummings, upon finding his eyeglasses. "Calloo callay!" He himself appeared and disappeared. "When through who-the-unotherish twilight updrops but his niblicks Sir Oral Né Ferdinand Joegesq," Cummings wrote to Pound. "Disarmed to the nonteeth by loseable scripture."[26]

He was forever falling apart, falling down, disintegrating, descending. "If I am not careful, I will be again checked by a bad nervous breakdown," he wrote to Williams. If he hadn't lost his glasses, he had broken them. "I had a very bad fall, a day or so ago, and smashed my glasses completely," he wrote to the critic Lewis Mumford. He very often got into fights. Cummings told this story: "'Joe' (I said to him) 'did you fall or were you pushed?' 'Whie-yuh, both.'" Some days, he could hardly see. But, he admitted, "my trouble with my eyes is more psychological than physical."[27] This got worse as he got older, and drunker. Writing—meaninglessly, endlessly—was all that held him together. Except that it didn't usually hold him together for long.

Days after *The New Yorker* published "Professor Sea Gull," a policeman found Gould outside a bar on 23rd Street, bleeding from his head while reciting the Oral History. He'd fallen and cracked his skull.[28] The next time he went to the hospital, he needed a blood transfusion. When the doctor asked him who might donate blood, Gould said, "Joe Mitchell."[29] Not long after that, he and Mitchell had a talk.

"I'm beginning to believe," Mitchell blurted out, "that the Oral History doesn't exist."

Mitchell didn't tell this story, about that talk, until 1964, when he was fifty-six and Gould was dead, in a second *New Yorker* profile, called "Joe Gould's Secret." Reading it was like watching DiMaggio play his best game ever. "Not only is it the best thing you have written," one reader wrote to Mitchell. "It is the best piece the New Yorker has ever published."[30]

The conversation Mitchell had had with Gould right after writing "Professor Sea Gull" went like this:

I knew as well as I knew anything that I had blundered upon the truth about the Oral History.

"My God!" I said. "It doesn't exist." I was appalled. "There isn't such a thing as the Oral History," I said. "It doesn't exist."

I stared at Gould, and Gould stared at me. His face was expressionless.[31]

And there ended the mystery of the longest book ever written and never read, an unpublished manuscript by the most important historian of the twentieth century, who wanted to do for history what Whitman did for poetry.

It didn't exist.

Or did it?

2

I am told this is the pen,
That it will write for me too

— PHILIP LEVINE,
"Joe Gould's Pen"

He wrote with a fountain pen. He filled it with ink he stole from inkstands at the post office. He carried it everywhere. "I wrote all day," he would write in his diary. Or, more often, "Wrote all day." Or, "Wrote all day. Went to the library."[1] Wrote, wrote, wrote.

There ought to be a DANGER sign. Writers tumble into this story and then they plummet. I have always supposed this to be because Gould suffered from graphomania—he could not stop writing—which is an illness, but seems more like something a writer might have to envy, which feels even rottener than envy usually does because Joe Gould was a toothless madman who slept in the street. You are envying a bum: Has it come to this, at last? But then you're relieved of the misery of that envy when you learn that everything he wrote was dreadful. Except, wait, that's worse, because then you have to ask: Maybe everything you write is dreadful, too? (WARN-ING: Do not ask that question from the bottom of a well.) But then, in one last twist, you find out that everything he wrote *never even existed.* Still, either way, honestly, it's depressing as hell.

So I got interested in knowing if any of it was true.

This began one winter. I was teaching a course called "What Is Biography?" to sophomores at Harvard. The point was to teach them how to research and write about other people's lives. For reading, I decided to assign not, strictly speak-ing, biographies, but instead books that I love and that say something cautionary and wise about the error of believing you can ever really know another person. (This happens to have been Gould's definition of insanity. "The fallacy of dividing people into sane and insane lies in the assumption that we really do touch other lives," he once wrote. "Hence I would judge the sanest man to be him who most firmly realizes the tragic isolation of humanity and pursues his essential purposes calmly.")[2] I'd included on the syllabus Julian Barnes's *The Sense of an Ending,* a devastatingly beautiful novel, and Joseph Mitchell's two profiles of Joe Gould: the delightful, Pickwickian 1942 story "Professor Sea Gull," and the much longer and much darker, Poe-like 1964 tale "Joe Gould's Secret." (In 1965, the two stories were published together as a book, later reissued by the Modern Library.)[3] Rereading Mitchell for class, I remembered something I'd forgotten: much of the story has to do with Harvard, beginning with the fact that Gould claimed to have graduated from the college in 1911 with a degree in history. Then there are the loose ends:

> In his breast pocket, sealed in a dingy envelope, he always carries a will bequeathing two-thirds of the manuscript to the Harvard Library and the other third to the Smithsonian Institution. "A couple of generations after I'm dead and gone," he likes to say, "the Ph.D.'s will start lousing through my work. Just imagine their surprise. 'Why, I'll be damned,' they'll say, 'this fellow was the most brilliant historian of the century.'"[4]

I stumbled. Whatever happened to that will? Had Mitchell seen it? Had Gould made it up? Had Mitchell made it up? For that matter, what about the Oral History? Mitchell hadn't seen it and said Gould had made it up, but maybe Mitchell had made that up. Wouldn't my students ask:

Isn't it possible that the Oral History had once existed and even that it still exists? Shouldn't someone *check*?

The day before class, I went to the library. I had this crazy idea: I wanted to find the lost archive.

Mitchell had gone to the library, too. He made sure to mention that later, when he was wondering how he could have gotten the story so wrong in 1942: What had he missed? He'd checked facts: "I had gone to the library of the Harvard Club and hunted through the reports of his class." He'd conducted interviews: "I had looked up around fifteen people and spoken on the phone to around fifteen others." He'd read parts of the Oral History that weren't oral (these, Gould explained, were the book's "essay chapters"):

> Now all I needed was one more thing, a look at the oral part of the Oral History, but that seemed to me essential. As far as I was concerned, the Oral History was Gould's reason for being, and if I couldn't quote from it, or even describe it first hand, I didn't see how I could write a Profile of him.[5]

But, what with one thing and another, Gould just couldn't put his hands on any of the necessary notebooks. He was pretty sure he'd stored most of them in the cellar of a friend's house, at a chicken farm on Long Island. Exasperated, Mitchell told

Gould he'd have to kill the piece: no Oral History, no story. Gould then began reciting whole chapters from memory ("Gould is afflicted with total recall," Mitchell explained):

> "This part of the Oral History is pretty gory," he said. "It is called 'Echoes from the Backstairs of Bellevue,' and it is divided into sections, under such headings as 'Spectacular Operations and Amputations,' 'Horrible Deaths,' 'Sadistic Doctors,' 'Alcoholic Doctors,' 'Drug-Addicted Doctors,' 'Women-Chasing Doctors,' 'Huge Tumors, Etc.,' and 'Strange Things Found During Autopsies.'"

Mitchell went ahead with the piece.

Reporting begins with listening; history begins with reading. The past is what's written down. It is very quiet; only people who can write make any sound at all. Gould wanted history to be noisier and more democratic, too: he wanted to record speech. Mitchell loved that idea. What if you could *report* history?

When Mitchell went to the library, everything checked out. But when I went to the library, and into the half-light of the archives, hardly anything checked out. And there's the chasm. I fell right into it.

·   ·   ·

Gould did not graduate from Harvard in 1911. Instead, he had a breakdown.[6] "There always was a queer streak in the Gould family," his sister's best friend said. The Goulds had come to New England in the 1630s, and they'd been strange for as long as anyone could remember. Gould was born in Massachusetts in 1889, and grew up in Norwood. In an office on the first floor of the family's house, his father, a doctor, saw patients every afternoon and evening. Dr. Gould was known to fly into rages, and so was Joseph. There was something terribly wrong with the boy. In his bedroom, he wrote all over the walls and all over the floor.[7] His sister, Hilda, found him so embarrassing, she pretended he didn't exist.[8] He kept seagulls as pets, or at least he said he had, and that he spoke their language: he would flap his hands, and skip, and caw.[9] He did this all his life. That's how he got the nickname "Professor Sea Gull."

Categories of illness are a function of history. It's not possible to diagnose a person who was born in 1889. That aside: hand flapping—and screeching and tiptoe walking—have since come to be understood as symptoms of autism.[10] Long ago, long before this distress had a name, wouldn't it have been remarkably clever for a boy who couldn't help but flap his hands and walk on tiptoe and screech to make up a story about how he was imitating a seagull, on purpose? It would have been so comforting, sense out of misery.

Whatever afflicted little Joe Gould, he had suffered from childhood, and it affected what he could do and what he couldn't. He started kindergarten at the age of five, but was sent home; he couldn't sit still. "I was too restless," he explained.[11] He was fidgety and undersized and nearsighted, and his thinking was sticky: he could master the smallest of details; he lost sight of much else. He was put in charge of the town's telephone service.[12] He found it hard to take tests. On his college entrance exams, he got four D's and one E (which is what F's used to be called).[13] He'd never have been admitted to Harvard if it hadn't been for the fact that both his father and his grandfather had gone there. (His grandfather also taught at the Harvard Medical School.) He was a Gould, and that was that. When he wrote a freshman essay called "Who I Am and Why I Came to Harvard," he explained, "I devoted four fifths of it to an account of my ancestors" because "I felt that this was the best explanation of myself."[14]

He was meant to become a doctor, like his father and grandfather. But when he started college, he was no more ready than he'd been for kindergarten. His parents kept him at home. Every day, he rode a train to Cambridge.[15] During his freshman year he failed both physics (once) and chemistry (twice). Medicine was out of the question. "Joseph was in the office yesterday, and we had a long talk," the dean informed Gould's father. "He has failed in practically all of his courses." He was put on academic probation. He hardly ever showed up for class. He was hapless. He went to the wrong French exam. In history, he failed to turn in his final paper.[16]

During his sophomore year, he managed to get off academic probation. "I am sure that you now have learned your lesson," the dean wrote to him. But he could not learn that lesson. His senior year, he fell apart and was expelled. "Under the circumstances," the chair of the college's Administrative Board wrote to Gould's father, "I do not think that the Board would be inclined to allow him to return to College until he has shown his ability to do continuous work in a satisfactory manner."[17]

His father was furious. "A College should never become so big or impersonal that it tends to break, rather than make a boy," he said, but that, he felt, was what happened to his son. Harvard had broken him. Also, he had struggled because he was a terrible notetaker. "He is left handed, very near sighted and not very strong," Gould's father explained. "He writes slowly because of this so can not take very good notes."[18]

He could hardly write.

I wrote all day. Wrote all day. Went to the library. Wrote all day. Wrote.

Wrote what?

3

little joe gould's quote oral
history unquote might (publishers note) be
entitled a wraith's
progress

—E. E. CUMMINGS

I decided to retrace his steps. If Gould had actually written a history of the world and then lost
it, maybe I could find it along the side of the road
somewhere, under a bush, in a gutter, down a
ditch. Maybe he left it somewhere, in a cabinet,
on a bookshelf, up in an attic, under a bed.

"I began work on the Oral History—Meo
Tempore—in October, 1916," Gould once explained. "Since then I have written a minimum of
a hundred sentences every day except for a period
of about four years when there was serious danger
of my going blind because of a weakened optic
nerve."[1] Nineteen sixteen. Or was it later? "GOT

DOWN TO REAL WORK ON ORAL HISTORY IN 1918," Joseph Mitchell wrote in his interview notes in 1942, but then he scratched in the margin, "later said 1917."[2] Another time Gould told a reporter, "I began my book in October, 1914," though he then added, "I didn't begin to work seriously, however, until 1916."[3] Nineteen fourteen. Or was it earlier? "I have known Mr. Joe Gould since 1911 or 1912," Edward J. O'Brien remembered. "It was in the latter year, I think, that he conceived the idea of his Oral History."[4] Nineteen twelve. I'd start with 1912.

O'Brien and Gould had overlapped at Harvard; O'Brien had dropped out with the idea that he could do a better job educating himself. In 1911, he introduced Gould to the poet and critic William Stanley Braithwaite, the literary editor of the *Boston Evening Transcript*.[5] Braithwaite hired O'Brien as a reviewer and, possibly, Gould, too. O'Brien and Braithwaite began planning to launch a magazine to be called *Poetry*. It was to be printed in Boston by the Four Seas Publishing Company, owned by Edmund R. Brown, another friend of Gould's. There seems to have been some suggestion that Gould would join the editorial staff.[6]

Or maybe Gould imagined that. Many of his relationships existed almost entirely in his head. He was smart, very smart, smart enough to have observed what meaningful relationships looked like—he was mannered, gentlemanly—but was generally unable to have them. So he made them up. He'd also bore into people, trying to get at their marrow, their blood and bloodline.

Braithwaite's father came from a wealthy British West Indian family; his mother was the daughter of a North Carolina slave. (It irked Braithwaite that he was known as "the Negro poet.") Gould found Braithwaite's ancestry fascinating. At the time, and for a very long time, sex between races was all he could think about.

"The problem of the Twentieth Century is the problem of the color line," W. E. B. Du Bois wrote in 1903.[7] The problem of the color line became the problem of Joe Gould's unraveling mind.

Two months after he was kicked out of Harvard, Gould began introducing himself as president of the Race Pride League. So far as I can tell, the Race Pride League did not exist. In June 1911, *The Boston Globe* published a collection of essays on the "race question," including one by Gould, who wrote:

> The man who opposes equal treatment for the colored race says, "If you ride on the same car with a negro you have to do business with him. If you do business with him you have to invite him to supper. If you invite him to supper he may marry your sister." After repeating this "logical" argument many times, he

adds, "And you know that you wouldn't care to marry a negress."

The way to defeat this argument, Gould concluded, was to disentangle racial equality from racial mixture: "It is inevitable that in time men of every color will enjoy equal privileges, and then it will be seen that racial equality is the surest guardian of race purity."[8]

His was the madness of whiteness. What the young, addled president of the Race Pride League proposed was a concocted *Plessy v. Ferguson*, an upended Garveyism: racial equality is inevitable and will assure racial purity, which is essential because racial mixture is unnatural. Even imagining sex across the color line, Gould believed, causes "an antipathy which is involuntary and is felt with such violence that it is comparable to the extreme repugnance some people have to snakes."[9] It's impossible not to suspect that he had been sexually rejected.

"I have been all the last college year on the verge of a collapse," Gould wrote Braithwaite a few months later, from Alberta: his parents had sent him on a five-hundred-mile walking trip across Canada. (Gould's mother was from Nova Scotia, and his uncle owned a ranch in British Columbia.) He talked to a lot of people while he was walking: trappers, ranchers, miners, missionaries, homesteaders. He also had sex. Later, in his diary, he told a story about meeting a woman who'd grown up in Alberta. "She said that she lost her virginity there to a man named Ross. I said, 'Well, I lost some one else's virginity there too.' "[10]

"I have been bucked off a Cayuse three times in succession," he wrote to Harvard when he got back. "My falls showed me how to stay on, and gave me a firmer seat in the saddle."[11] He was not readmitted. He went home to Norwood to live with his parents and his little sister. He became the Enumerator of the Census. He embarked on a racial survey of the town's inhabitants. He delivered a lecture called "Why Certain Races Are Disliked."[12] And he began writing down the things people say, especially about who they like and who they don't.

I finished my day in the archives and went to class. I brought in stacks of photocopies of Gould's undergraduate files: his academic records, his transcripts, his letters to deans and professors, recounting his adventures, spouting his theories, begging for money. My students and I hunched over a seminar table and peered at his scrawl. The more we read, the sadder the story got.

In 1913, Gould again petitioned for readmission to Harvard. When that failed, he had the idea of applying to the graduate school. "I think you could at any rate give me credit for persistence," he complained. Then he floated the idea of writing a thesis in history to make up his missing credits. No one on the faculty wanted to work with him.[13]

Class ended. But I found that I could not stop searching.

Gould told O'Brien about the Oral History, and O'Brien began giving him money to support his work; that's why O'Brien was pretty certain about the year Gould began: 1912. In Chicago, the poet Harriet Monroe got word of O'Brien and Braithwaite's plans to launch a poetry magazine and decided to beat them to it; she called her magazine *Poetry*, leaving O'Brien and Braithwaite to call theirs *The Poetry Journal*. Braithwaite was editor, O'Brien and Brown assistant editors. Gould's name did not appear anywhere in the inaugural issue.[14] In 1913, Braithwaite began editing an annual poetry anthology, and in 1914, O'Brien did the same for fiction with *Best Short Stories*, which he edited for the rest of his life. It's still printed, every year.

O'Brien moved to England; Gould sent him a wad of his manuscript. Among Gould's many excuses for having misplaced hundreds of his notebooks is that O'Brien never returned them. Quite possibly, that's true. Whatever notebooks O'Brien once had are gone; after his death, his papers were destroyed.[15]

I started looking every place I could think to

look, for anything Gould had left behind: not just the Oral History, anything at all. It turns out that a graphomaniac is an unnervingly irresistible research subject. Gould was almost impossibly easy to trace. Every time I checked another archive, another vault, another library, it'd have sheaves of letters. And then there were the diaries.

Gould kept a diary in the same kind of black-and-speckled-white, dime-store composition notebooks that he used to write the Oral History. For years, the artist Harold Anton kept ten volumes of Gould's diaries at his studio in Greenwich Village. "I know where Joe Gould keeps his Oral History and I will take you to their hiding place," a man named Jack Levitz wrote to Joseph Mitchell in 1964.[16] "As I suspected, 'their hiding place' is Harold Anton's studio," Mitchell wrote in a note to himself, after he spoke to Levitz on the phone.[17] Mitchell had already seen those notebooks: they were probably part of what convinced him that the Oral History didn't exist. After "Joe Gould's Secret" was published, Anton sold the notebooks to a Village impresario, who sold them to an archivist at New York University, who, after skimming them, decided that Mitchell was a dupe ("Joe recognized a mark when he saw one") and Gould was a fraud ("Joe Gould lied about his work; the quality of what remains is dreadful; and he has no place in literary history").[18]

Maybe so. Or maybe not. Opening those notebooks expecting the Oral History and finding only a diary, it's easy to conclude that, all along, Gould had only ever been writing a diary, and passing it off as something more. It's also easy, then, not to read the diary carefully: Why bother?

I went to see the diaries as soon as I found out about them, cursing my curiosity. I brought a camera. I filled out a call slip and sat at a table. Gould's notebooks came out from the stacks, one by one, stained and blotted. The ten surviving volumes of Gould's diary fill more than eight hundred pages. I photographed every page.

The first diary begins on the first of the year. "New Years found me at Slater Brown's," he wrote, in black ink now faded. "I took a bath and wrote."[19]

Wrote what? Not the diary. Something else. Instead of proving that the Oral History never existed, the diaries suggest exactly the opposite. Also, Gould's diaries are only disappointing if you're looking for the Oral History. As diaries, as a record of a life, they're often dull, but they're also cluttered with detail and full of speech. One day, Gould traveled to Connecticut:

> I went to the Grand Central. I could not phone from there. I took a train. The man who sat besides me handled an argument with a man who tried to steal his baggage space. He loaned me his magazines. I talked with him. He had travelled widely. He knew much about

cattle. He was interested when I told him about seeing oxen shod. When the train took a turn at South Norwalk he said, "From now on it will get more civilized."[20]

On the train ride home, I tried transcribing the diaries, squinting at my photographs. "I got up late. I ate at Stewarts. I had an invitation from Doctor Alan Gregg. I wrote."[21] Gregg, a psychiatrist, had been a member of Gould's class at Harvard. His papers are housed at the National Library of Medicine. I emailed the archivist there and asked him if he'd be willing to check the "G" correspondence file in Gregg's papers for anything from Joe Gould ("You mean *the* Joe Gould?" people would ask). An hour later, the archivist emailed me PDFs of letters in that familiar hand: "My dear Doctor Gregg . . ."[22]

I pictured it like this: I'd dip those letters and pages torn from the diaries in a bath of glue and water—the black ink would begin to bleed— and I'd paste them over an armature I'd built out of Gould's empty cigarette boxes, rolled up old *New Yorker*s, and seagull feathers. I called my papier-mâché *White Man (Variation)*.

In 1913, when Gould was twenty-four, he began writing to Charles B. Davenport, the leader of the American eugenics movement.[23] Gould sent letters to eminences all over the world; very few people ever answered. He once tried to recruit Franz Boas to a campaign he was waging to aid Albania.[24] "I think we have seen sufficiently clearly what that kind of 'help' leads to," Boas wrote back. "You will therefore excuse me if I do not join in an enterprise which seems to me radically wrong." Then he dropped the correspondence.[25] You can usually tell, when you get the kind of letter Gould wrote, that you are dealing with someone unhinged. Davenport couldn't tell.

Gould must have first learned about Davenport's work in 1910 when he took a class called "Variation and Heredity" with William E. Castle, who had trained with Davenport. "I enjoyed his course," Gould wrote to Davenport. "Although I did not distinguish myself in it as I was on the verge of the breakdown which sent me out to Alberta."[26]

Davenport had earned a Ph.D. in zoology at Harvard in 1892 and taught there until 1899, when he published *Statistical Methods with Special Reference to Biological Variation*. In 1904, he founded the Station for Experimental Evolution in Cold Spring Harbor, New York. In 1910, he opened the Eugenics Record Office, and in *Eugenics* he defined its work as "the science of human improvement by better breeding."[27]

"The race question," Gould wrote Davenport, "is largely one of eugenics." People fall in love across the color line and other people don't love them back. "The glorification of romantic love seems to be one of the chief obstacles to public acceptance of eugenics," Gould wrote. He had gotten an idea. He would write a very long book, an epic novel, a fictive History of America. "It seems to me that a new fiction is desirable which shall sympathize with the point of view that outside choice might bring greater happiness in wedlock than irresponsible and perhaps momentary fancies of youth."[28] He wrote out the beginning of the book, some early chapters, and sent it to Davenport.

"It is interesting as literature," Davenport wrote back. "Do you wish the copy returned?" Gould said no. All that survives is Gould's description: "I have in mind the writing of a fictitious genealogy of the descendants of a slave brought here in 1619, with an attempt to show all the phases of degeneration or progress which resulted from the introduction of the Negro into this country."[29]

He never said what he planned to call it. I think of it as *Un-Beloved*.

4

"We offer . . . this rare and original manuscriptum being the first and only extant draft of Sowerby's History of—what was it you said you was writing a history of, Mr. Sowerby?"

"I am writing a history, sir, of irrelevant and unimportant details."

—MAXWELL ANDERSON AND
HAROLD HICKERSON,
Gods of the Lightning

He picked and pulled at this question, the race question. Variation and heredity, better breeding, sex across the color line, the racial nature of disgust, and of love. He turned to history, to ancestry, to biology, to genealogy. He wrote and he wrote.

"I think it would add to the interest of your fictitious genealogy if you would include an intermarriage with an Indian," Davenport suggested. "So many of our degenerate families trace back to an Indian ancestor."[1]

"My opinion is that the Indian strain has been a helpful one," Gould ventured.[2]

He decided he disagreed with Davenport's ideas about racial hierarchy. One reason Gould was interested in eugenics was because he'd come to understand—maybe his failures had helped him to see—that he hadn't earned the extravagant opportunities he'd been given in life; he'd inherited them. If, when asked to write an essay on "Who I Am and Why I Came to Harvard," all he could say was that he was a Gould, what was the lesson there? "It seems to me that one error is commonly made in speaking of heredity which is well illustrated by the descendants of Jonathan Edwards so many of whom were eminent," Gould wrote Davenport. "Their eminence was due, it seems to me, not as much to inherited ability as to inherited opportunity."[3] Consider Edwards's grandson, Aaron Burr: he'd inherited not talent, Gould thought, but chance. And so had he.

He studied hatred. He watched the people whose ancestries he'd traced: some hated blacks, some hated Jews. He developed a theory about "race prejudice": "I have examined over a hundred cases of antipathy among people whose personal equation I knew, and I made a startling discovery which I believe will be borne out by further evidence," Gould wrote Davenport. "I found that those who had physical repugnance to the Jew had no feeling against the Negro, and vice-versa." From this, Gould had concluded that "the Jew and the Negro are physically and temperamentally antipodes, being opposites in their mental qualities, vices and virtues. For this reason it would be perfectly natural for them to be disliked by opposite sets of people." He wished to conduct further experiments: he wanted to test his theory in the field.[4]

Davenport had no interest in Gould's ideas about inequality of opportunity or race prejudice; what he wanted was help documenting the degenerative effects of the darker races on the whiter ones. He believed that the whiteness of the United States could be preserved by restricting immigration and banning miscegenation; he also hoped to eliminate the feeble-minded and the insane by forced sterilization. He proposed visiting Gould on his next trip to Boston.[5] Gould invited him to speak at Harvard, where Gould was trying to make up his missing credits by taking exams.[6] He wanted him to speak at the Cosmopolitan Club, whose members included students from China, Germany, England, Canada, Japan, France, India, Cuba, Hawaii, Italy, Brazil, Greece, Mexico, New Zealand, the Philippines, Puerto Rico, Siam, and Spain, and whose faculty sponsor was Gould's heredity professor, William Castle.[7] Gould also told Davenport that he was about to become the editor of a new, cosmopolitan magazine, *Four Seas*, whose features would include "the life-story in serial numbers of Plenyono Gbe Wolo," a Liberian who had entered Harvard that fall; he invited Davenport to write a column called "The Newer Race."[8]

Gould never became the editor of anything.[9] But he did write for *The Nation*, and for *The Crisis*, the magazine of the NAACP.[10] He helped Upton Sinclair collect essays for an anthology called *The Cry for Justice*.[11] He "lectured on behalf of educating the poor southern Negroes."[12] In the summer of 1914, he spoke at the Sagamore Conference, a social justice gathering convened by Jane Addams.[13] There he met a young progressive reformer from New York named Frances Perlstein. At the end of that summer, he later said, he became engaged to her.[14]

Most of all, he gathered evidence for his study of ancestry. The Oral History began as a Harvard senior thesis, later aborted, and turned into an epic novel about race, based on a genealogical chart. It might have been called *Roots*. "I have made some beginning toward my collection of pedigrees, to be welded into the fictitious genealogy of a Negro slave," he reported to Davenport in 1915, when he gave a lecture on family history before the Boston Negro Business League. "There will be enough sugar-coating of interesting history to suggest to the members the desirability of collecting their family records," he promised. Lectures like these, he explained, offered "a good time for starting a eugenic propaganda among colored people."[15]

In April 1915, Gould was arrested outside the Tremont Theatre in Boston, for protesting D. W. Griffith's *Birth of a Nation*. "Mr. Gould has made a study of every nation, the people and their lives," the *Boston Herald* reported.[16] A lot of people were arrested that night protesting Griffith's tribute to the Ku Klux Klan. Nearly all of them were black Bostonians. Gould was the only one who was named in the paper.

Three months after Gould was arrested for protesting *Birth of a Nation*, he applied for work at Davenport's Eugenics Record Office. His application is filed with the Eugenics Record Office Papers, at the American Philosophical Society in Philadelphia.

"Has done some historical writing," one of his interviewers noted. "Is a radical in politics." Another wrote down, "Spells of depression . . . violent temper." Ought he be allowed to breed? "Glasses at 17," Gould wrote on his application form, noting his inherited defects. He was under-sized: five foot four, 115 pounds. He was only twenty-five years old but had already lost most of his hair. On the other hand: "Good teeth." He supplied the required pedigree chart. He traced the trait of his "temper" back through three generations: the madness of the Goulds.[17]

He was hired and sent to North Dakota on a six-month assignment to conduct measurements on Mandan Indians. Using calipers, he was supposed to measure their arms, legs, heads, and noses; using a top designed by Milton Bradley—a child's toy, but put to a new purpose by eugenicists—he was to record skin color.[18] The idea was to attach differently colored cards to the top and then spin it, switching one card for another until the color of the spinning top matched that of the subject's skin.[19] This, *this:* this was the madness of the color line.

Once Gould got to Minnesota he told Davenport that he wished his Eugenics Record Office training had included information about venereal disease.[20] (He may have contracted a form of syphilis, known at the time as "general paresis of the insane," that eventually infected his brain: that would explain his later psychosis and dementia.[21] It's impossible to say. And there are other explanations for his disorder.) "The life of the Indian is more influenced by sex than ours," Gould reported: he'd met a man named Four Times ("an allusion to four successive acts of sexual intercourse") and a woman named Big Vagina. Then, too: "One man was named Goes-to-bed-with-a-man."[22] Years later, when Gould was floridly mad and living in Greenwich Village, he'd turn up drunk at parties, strip naked, stand on a table, demand a ruler, and measure his penis.[23]

In his work among the Indians, he encountered many obstacles. It was fifty degrees below freezing; travel was difficult; he fell off a horse; the shades on his set of Bradley tops were all wrong: "the red used for Negroes is too dark for the Indian."[24] Also, the people didn't trust him; they refused to be measured. "It is natural that the Indians regard as uncanny what they can not understand," he wrote Davenport.[25] But they had abundant reason to refuse. The work Gould was doing was to help the U.S. government resolve a series of lawsuits involving the selling off of thirteen hundred parcels of reservation land by "mixed-bloods" whose authority to sell that land was disputed by "full-bloods": Gould, with a child's plaything, was supposed to determine which Indians were reddest.[26]

He wrote to Harvard asking for a course catalog.[27] He needed only one more class to graduate. "In my preoccupation with trying to be an Injun," he wrote to the dean, "I do not wish to forget the academic life." He wished to study Tolstoy or, better yet, the history of the Jews.[28] "My racial work is going on in such a way that I do not want to take up college work too remote in subject from it," he reported, asking to be allowed to take the examination in a zoology class on race mixture taught by the anthropologist Earnest Albert Hooton.[29] Meanwhile, he kept up his work as a book reviewer. He condemned *America's Greatest Problem: The Negro*, by R. W. Shufeldt

("He adopts any pseudo-scientific work which strengthens his case, and quotes with ghoulish glee newspaper clippings about Negro crime"), and praised Carter G. Woodson's history of black education ("one colored man at least sees that the hope of his race lies in the appeal to history").[30] Then he wrote to W. E. B. Du Bois, inviting the NAACP to form an alliance with the Society of American Indians.[31] Du Bois did not write back.

Gould returned to Harvard and read with Hooton.[32] Hooton had no use for people he called "ethnomaniacs" who "talk of the psychological characteristics of this or that race as if they were objective tangible properties, scientifically demonstrated." There was no evidence whatever to support that position, and in any case, "Most if not all peoples are racially mixed."[33]

Gould passed Hooton's exam, changed his mind about race mixture, got his degree, and moved to New York, where he wrote an essay about the institutional care of the insane,[34] bunked in flophouses, begged for handouts, and began telling everyone who would listen that he was the most brilliant historian of the twentieth century, that he was writing a history of the world, and that it would last as long as the English language.

5

He knew the book, it was in his mind entirely, and
in fact why write it?

— PATRICIA HIGHSMITH,
"The Man Who Wrote Books in His Head"

Two writers guard an archive. One writes fiction; the other writes fact. To get past them,
you have to figure out which is which. Joseph
Mitchell said that Gould made things up. But
Gould said that Mitchell did. Who's right?

In 1964, in "Joe Gould's Secret," Mitchell explained that, in 1942, right after "Professor Sea
Gull" was published, he'd come to believe that
Gould had only imagined that he'd written the
longest book ever written: "He very likely went
around believing in some hazy, self-deceiving,
self-protecting way that the Oral History did
exist." Mitchell said he understood Gould, and

wanted to protect him, so he decided to keep his secret. He could see very well how just this sort of thing could happen, how a man could come to believe that he had written a book when in fact he had not—"He had it all in his head, and any day now he was going to start getting it down"— because he'd done the same thing himself. For years, Mitchell had been planning to write an autobiographical novel. He thought about it all the time. "Sometimes, in the course of a subway ride, I would write three or four chapters," he wrote. "But the truth is, I never actually wrote a word of it."[1]

Mitchell didn't forgive Gould because he didn't need to; he didn't blame him. It's the grace of this act that carries force: Mitchell's compassion, wrapping little Joe Gould in his great cloak.

Gould, though, said that it was Mitchell who made things up, and he did blame him, and he didn't forgive him. After reading "Professor Sea Gull," he wrote Mitchell, "I feel as if I was only a figment of your imagination."[2] Mitchell asked Gould what it was in the profile that wasn't true. "He thought about it for a while and said, 'I never bought a radio and kicked it to pieces.'"[3] But Gould's objections ran deeper. He considered "Professor Sea Gull" a work of fiction. In 1943, he told Lewis Mumford that it was "one of the best short stories of 1942."[4] And in 1945, when the profile was reprinted in an anthology of short stories, he told Mitchell that he was pleased, since "this is a sort of recognition that the piece is fiction."[5]

Gould was not wrong. Mitchell admitted to Gould that he made up facts. "He said his account of the Mayor of Fulton Fish Market was largely fictionalized," Gould carefully noted in his diary.[6] And it's since come out that Mitchell sometimes invented quotes and even whole scenes, and once wrote an entire profile about a man who did not exist.[7] Gould did not consider this kind of thing a kindness.

But Gould and Mitchell agreed about one thing: when Mitchell looked in the mirror, he saw Gould. "He has pictured me as the sort of person he would like to be," Gould said.[8] And Mitchell, asked why he was so fascinated by Gould, said, "Because he is me."[9]

"Joe Gould's Secret" is a confession, and it's also a defense of invention. Mitchell took something that wasn't beautiful—the sorry fate of a broken man—and made it beautiful, a fable about art. "The Joe Gould piece is so beautiful and moving that no one could have written it but W. B. Yeats," a fellow *New Yorker* writer told Mitchell.[10] "Joe Gould's Secret" is the best story many people have ever read. Its truth is, in a Keatsian sense, its beauty, its beauty its truth.

I by now sorely regretted having gone to the

library, that first day, to see if any of it was true, in the drearier, empirical, Baconian sense: "Doth any man doubt, that if there were taken out of men's minds vain opinions, flattering hopes, false valuations, imaginations as one would and the like, but it would leave the minds of a number of men poor shrunken things, full of melancholy and indisposition and unpleasing to themselves?"[11] The more I learned about Joe Gould, the uglier it got.

"Not an alcoholic, not psychopathic," Mitchell wrote in his notes when he interviewed Gould in 1942.[12] Why believe him? Why de-fang him? "I thought of Joe as a kind of hero," Mitchell said.[13] So did Gould's friends. E. E. Cummings once asked Gould how he reconciled his faith in a benevolent God with the miserableness of his own life. Gould considered the question:

A mood of self-pity came over me. It was hard to be hungry and shabby and worried over finance, and to be deceived by friends and in such a mental state that I, who had smoked the peace-pipe with Water Chief and ought to be strong and honest above all other whites, found myself completely unnerved and untrustworthy when deprived of cigarettes. At the moment I could not answer him. But when I pondered the matter over the answer came. I have not had a hard time. A pinched stomach, a humiliating situation to my pride,

and mental torment have never stayed my pen.
I have always been able to do that which I felt
was worth doing. What cause have I to rail at
fate?[14]

And that's the way modernist writers and artists tended to regard the situation. Torment had
never stayed his pen: Gould was an artist, a bohemian, suffering for his art, suffering for *their* art,
suffering for all art. *Because he is me.*

Not me.

This difference is partly a function of time. A
century on, Gould looks bleak, his mental illness
looks serious, and modernism looks fairly vicious,
actually. Gould's friends saw a man suffering for
art; I saw a man tormented by rage. To me, his
suffering didn't look romantic and his rage didn't
look harmless. But the difference is even more a
matter of evidence. I have never listened to Joe
Gould call out, as he strutted along the streets
of New York flapping like a seagull, "Scree-eek!
Scree-eek! Scree-eek!"[15] I couldn't hear him. But
in the stillness of the archives, I could read him.
And Mitchell could not. All those letters that I
found in archives all over the country? They
weren't in archives when Mitchell was writing
about Gould; they were stashed in people's desks
and closets and attics. Mitchell met one man; I
met another.

And I wished, I dearly wished, that I could

let him be. But I'd gotten awfully worried. The defense of invention has its limits. Believing things that aren't real and writing fiction are acts of imagination: delusion and illusion. But passing off fiction as fact isn't an act of imagination; it's an act of deception. And with deception, someone usually gets hurt. Gould got hurt, Mitchell got hurt. I figured they weren't the only ones.

I also still thought I might find the Oral History. Because a man who as a boy runs the town's telephone service and as a young man serves as the Enumerator of the Census and collects the pedigrees of everyone he meets seems not unlikely to have recorded in dime-store composition notebooks everything that was ever said to him. That the Oral History had never been found didn't convince me that it had never existed. Very little of what most people write is saved, and nearly all of what is said is lost. That's why Gould was writing the thing in the first place. "I am trying to preserve as much detail as I can about the normal life of every day people," he wrote, because "as a rule, history does not deal with such small fry."[16] Gould wanted to save the ordinary; the ordinary are very hard to save. But when "Professor Sea Gull" appeared, it made Gould famous. ("They had read about me in the New Yorker," he wrote in his diary about people who sought him out.)[17] And what famous people write is saved.

·   ·   ·

I had started searching in the winter. In the spring, Joseph Mitchell's papers arrived at the New York Public Library.

They'd been in family hands since his death. They'd only just been picked up from his daughter's house, in forty-two boxes. They hadn't yet been cataloged, and the library was about to ship them to a contractor for sorting and preservation. I asked if I could take a look first.

Joe Gould spent a lot of time in the library at the corner of 42nd and Fifth, writing. The staff took to calling him "the poor man's Shakespeare."[18] I thought of him while I sat at a table in the Manuscripts and Archives Division, waiting. The semester had ended and I'd taken a train from Boston. I pictured Gould at a table nearby, hunched over his notebook, blotting his ink.

Mitchell kept his Gould material in three big boxes: interview notes, receipts, drafts, proofs, and letters from readers. I keep my yarn in a drawer, and I don't know how this happens, but every time I open that drawer, the different balls of yarn have gotten all tangled up, and before I can knit anything I have to spend hours untangling knots and unraveling skeins. Those boxes were like that drawer. I sat at my table, opened the first box, and began untangling, one knot at a time.

In 1964, in "Joe Gould's Secret," Mitchell said that he'd tried and tried to read the Oral History while interviewing Gould in 1942, without success, but that he'd taken its existence on faith because he did a great deal of other research about Gould's life and everything else checked out. Only after "Professor Sea Gull" appeared did he change his mind about the existence of the Oral History. This came about because Gould kept hounding him for money and attention and Mitchell, exasperated, arranged for Gould to meet with Max Perkins, an editor at Scribner's—Perkins edited Fitzgerald, Hemingway, and Wolfe—and when Gould kept on failing to deliver to Perkins any "oral parts" of the Oral History, and said he would only publish it posthumously, Mitchell confronted him with his suspicion that the history did not exist. Mitchell then decided, out of generosity and empathy, not to tell anyone the truth. He revisited this decision in August 1957, when, two days after Gould's death, Edward Gottlieb, editor of the *Long Island Press*, asked Mitchell to join a search committee to look for the Oral History. This is how Mitchell ends "Joe Gould's Secret":

> Joe Gould wasn't even in his grave yet, he wasn't even cold yet, and this was no time to be telling his secret. It could keep. Let them go ahead and look for the Oral History, I thought. After all, I thought, I could be wrong. Hell, I thought—and the thought made me smile—maybe they'll find it.

Gottlieb repeated his question, this time a little impatiently. "You will be on the committee, won't you?" he asked.

"Yes," I said, continuing to play the role I had stepped into the afternoon I discovered that the Oral History did not exist—a role that I am only now stepping out of. "Of course I will."[19]

This is true in spirit, but it's not actually true. Mitchell did not do a great deal of research in 1942 on Gould's early life. He did call Charles Davenport: Davenport told him that Gould was "erratic" and did not have a scientific mind. Mitchell did not type his notes with Davenport, since the call was so short, and he didn't use any of it. Other than Davenport, Mitchell's only real source for Gould's life before New York was Gould, who was not forthcoming. "Gould is not particularly communicative about what he calls his pre–Oral History life," Mitchell wrote in a draft of "Professor Sea Gull"—a line a *New Yorker* editor cut before the piece went to press.[20] In 1942, Gould gave Mitchell the names of people who had read the Oral History; Mitchell did not seek them out. I don't think he was especially interested in reading it; he was interested in listening to Gould.[21] (It made a better story in 1942 if the Oral History existed. It made a better story in 1964 if it did not.) Mitchell also heard a lot about Gould in 1942 that he did not report in "Professor Sea Gull." He heard about a man named William Allen who believed Gould's "oral history a fake" and that the "reason he is so secretive about it is that there is nothing there." As far as I can tell, Mitchell did not interview Allen. A woman named Mary Holt, who knew Gould well, told Mitchell, "Some people think he is a monster."[22] That didn't make it into the piece, either.

It is true, absolutely true, horribly true, that after "Professor Sea Gull" appeared, Gould hounded Mitchell. It must have been awful, much worse than Mitchell ever let on. Gould had a terrible way of turning on people. But it's not true that not until after the profile appeared did Gould begin saying the Oral History could only be published posthumously; Gould had been saying that since the 1920s. Nor is it true that Mitchell introduced Gould to Perkins: that introduction was made in April 1943 by the writer Slater Brown, whose kindnesses to Gould included feeding him dinner six nights a week. Nor is it true that, after Gould's death in August 1957, Mitchell participated in a search initiated by Gottlieb. Instead, beginning in October of that year, Mitchell began his own search for the Oral History. It seems as though nearly all of the research Mitchell said he'd done in 1942, including going to the library of the Harvard Club, he did not in 1942 but between 1957 and 1963, when he not only researched Gould's life but also searched for the lost manuscripts, tirelessly. He looked everywhere (and kept careful receipts). In July 1959, he went to Norwood to visit the house where Gould had grown up and to interview the woman who lived there. She told him that when she bought the house, in 1946, she'd found in the attic, under the eaves, "trunks of books" and dusty cardboard boxes tied with string, full of "report cards, school papers, compositions." She didn't know what to do with them. She tried to find a Gould family relative; no luck. She consulted an antiques dealer; the stuff was worthless. Finally, she told Mitchell, "I took it out to the Norwood Public Dump and dumped it." The only thing of Gould's that she kept, she said, was an old Edison phonograph.[23]

Still, it was a gamble to say that the Oral History didn't exist when he couldn't prove it. He clipped out of newspapers the obituaries of people who knew Gould well. They died off one by one. E. E. Cummings died in 1962, William Carlos Williams in 1963. *The New Yorker* published "Joe Gould's Secret" in two parts, in September 1964. And then what Mitchell must have feared happened: people who'd known Gould began writing him letters and calling his office to tell him that he was wrong. "Odds and ends of the ORAL HISTORY did exist," one man wrote to Mitchell in October.[24] "You were too hard on Joe," another man wrote in November. "When you became involved in Joe Gould's life in 1942 and onward, his composition books may well have contained only re-polished essays, but in the late 1920's and early 1930s, when I was first friendly with him, he daily jotted down the interests, events, sayings and occurrences of the day."[25] To everyone who wrote to tell him the Oral History existed, Mitchell sent characteristically courteous, lovely replies: "I wish I had had this information when I wrote the second Profile, for I certainly would've made use of it," he wrote, "and if I ever write another article about Joe Gould, which I may do, I'd like very much to have a talk with you about him."[26]

If there'd been one stray letter, or two, they'd have been easy to dismiss. Odds and ends, occurrences of the day: Maybe what those readers had seen were volumes of the diary? But there was more.

One letter that arrived that fall was from a woman named Florence Lowe who had known Gould when he first moved to New York. "My husband and I were his closest friends," Lowe told Mitchell. Gould had given her one of his notebooks in 1923, as a going-away present when she was sailing for Europe. Mitchell asked if he could see it. Lowe mailed Mitchell the notebook in December. She didn't hear from him for three months, so she wrote again, asking him if he'd received it. He wrote back and said he had gotten it, and wondered whether he might keep it to give to the New York Public Library. She said sure. "If you ever need any pre-Village Gould, let me know," she added. "I've got trunks full!"[27] He did not ask for more.

The notebook Florence Lowe sent Joseph Mitchell in 1964 reached the New York Public Library a half a century later, neatly filed with Mitchell's papers along with the envelope she sent it in. The notebook is dated 1922. It is titled "Meo Tempore. Seventh Version. Volume II." Sitting at a desk in the Manuscripts and Archives Reading Room, I laid that notebook flat, gripped with an uncertain fear.

Gould had filled only a few pages before he gave the notebook away. But it does have talk in it, snatches of conversation, like this:

> When Mr. Coan was a reporter, he heard President Taft speak to a group of suffrag- ists. He happened to mention some man who opposed that measure, and they hissed, not intending disrespect to him, but to show their disapproval of that particular gent. Taft seemed quite huffed about it. He stopped his speech off short to say, "If you women desire a share in the representation of government, you should learn self-control."[28]

This isn't much. It's not uninteresting, but its worth would seem to depend on whether or not there's a vast amount more of it. *It will have future value as a storehouse of information.*[29] Still, it *is* Oral History, not a diary, not a reporter's notebook: a historian's notebook. I pictured Mitchell at his desk at *The New Yorker*, reading "Meo Tempore," his head in his hands.

It's a piece of lore that after Mitchell wrote "Joe Gould's Secret," he never wrote another story ever again, not anything about Gould, not anything about anything, even though he went to his office at *The New Yorker* every day for more than three decades, until his death in 1996. That's not quite true, but it's nearly true. In the Keatsian sense. It's as if he'd been silenced by Joe Gould's curse.

I picked up the notebook. I turned the page.

"Meo Tempore. Seventh Version. Volume II" also contains an essay, written in Gould's unmistakable hand. It is titled "Insanity." I peered at the page of white with veins of blue. And there I read:

If we could see ourselves as we really are, life would be insupportable.[30]

PART TWO

Miss Savage

6

When you meet a member of the Ku Klux Klan,
Walk right up and hit him like a natural man.

—ROBERT LINCOLN POSTON,
"When You Meet a Member of the Ku Klux Klan"

Insanity is a topic of peculiar interest to me,"
Gould wrote in "Meo Tempore" in 1922.[1] He
had toured New York's insane asylums as part of
the training he received at the Eugenics Record
Office.[2] He'd measured heads and spun colored tops.[3] "I could very easily imagine myself
locked up as a maniac," he admitted. "Consider
the woman I met at Central Islip," an asylum
on Long Island: sometimes she thought she was
a cat; sometimes she thought she was a mouse.
"Is there really much difference between her and
a sane person, after all?" Gould asked. "We all
spend our lives, chasing into darkness."[4]

Gould had moved to New York in 1916 and had very quickly gone broke. "I should have gone home," he wrote. "However Frances Perlstein went into the hospital to be operated on and I lived on tea and cheap cigarettes to be near her."[5] Whatever Gould's relationship with Perlstein had been, it soon ended; Perlstein married another man.[6] Gould wrote to William Stanley Braithwaite to ask if he might help out with Braithwaite's anthology of American poetry, telling him that he was keen to write about his experiences "reading perfectly pallid poems of prostitution to Motorcycle Billy on an Indian reservation, and making him weep."[7] Braithwaite said no.

In 1917, when the United States entered the war, Gould tried to enlist in the army: he was rejected three times. His father, a captain in the medical reserve, was stationed in Ohio; he tried to get Gould a job teaching at the University of Ohio. Gould wrote to Harvard asking for a copy of his transcript to support his application.[8] He didn't get the job.

In New York, he was hired as a reporter for the *Evening Mail*.[9] That didn't last long: he didn't get along with his editor, or with the other reporters, either. "Some police-court reporters burned several volumes of my history because they resented a man's having intellectual interests," he later claimed. "It was a great blow to me."[10] In 1919, penniless, Gould went back to Norwood. That year, his father died suddenly of septicemia; Gould fell apart.[11] After he got better, he tried living in Boston for a while but ended up back in New York. "I had a pretty bad nervous breakdown and am just getting on my feet again," he wrote at the beginning of 1921, the year that he began describing himself as a historian.[12] He mailed Edward J. O'Brien another chunk of the Oral History, "perhaps a fiftieth of the magnum opus."[13] He told Braithwaite, "I have found the right task for me to do."[14] He began signing his letters, "Retrospectively, Joe."[15]

"I am having a great time in New York," Gould wrote to a cousin in 1923. "I am not making much money. However, I am meeting all sorts of interesting people. They are mainly artists." He was closest to the writer John Dos Passos and the sculptor Gaston Lachaise. "One of my most interesting stunts is visiting Negro Harlem," he wrote. He'd settled in Greenwich Village, but he spent a great deal of time uptown, eavesdropping on what Alain Locke called the "New Negro Movement," the Harlem Renaissance. "The people are trying to do two things," Gould reported. "They are trying to get our civilization. They are trying to build one of their own." It was history, unfolding: he took everything down. "I know a very attractive sculptress there named Augusta Savage," he went on. "She also writes poetry, but I don't hold that against her."[16] *Retrospectively, Joe.*

. . .

Augusta Savage was born Augusta Fells in Green Cove Springs, Florida, in 1892, the seventh of fourteen children. Both of her parents had been born into slavery. Her father was a minister who earned his living painting houses. Her mother didn't know how to read. Five of her brothers and sisters died as children. As a girl, she loved to sculpt out of clay. "At the mud pie age, I began to make 'things' instead of mud pies," she said. She loved to make ducks. "I liked the way their tails perked up in the back." Reverend Fells considered sculpture idolatrous. "My father licked me five or six times a week and almost whipped all the art out of me." She'd wanted to be a nurse, an obstetrical nurse. Instead, she married when she was fifteen. She had a baby, a daughter, Irene, and was widowed. Then she married a carpenter named James Savage. She left him. In 1921, she moved to New York to study at Cooper Union. She and her daughter, then fourteen, lived at 228 West 138th Street.[17] Savage supported them by taking in laundry. She told people that Irene was her little sister, pretended that she was a decade younger than she was, and never admitted to her first two marriages. W. E. B. Du Bois, in an essay in *The Crisis*, referred to her as "Miss Savage."[18] That's what everyone called her.

She had almond eyes, a delicate elegance, and an extraordinarily gentle voice.[19] "I fell in love with her at first sight," Gould wrote.[20] She was slender and long-limbed. She was taller; he was older.[21] He met her on March 21, 1923, at a poetry night at the 135th Street branch of the New York Public Library: "Original poems were read by Countee P. Cullen, Eric Waldron, Augusta Savage, Langston Hughes, Sadie Peterson and Gwendolyn Bennett."[22]

She soon abandoned poetry for art. The 135th Street library commissioned her to make a portrait of Du Bois. This led to a commission to make a bust of Marcus Garvey. Through Garvey, Savage met Robert Lincoln Poston, secretary-general of Garvey's Universal Negro Improvement Association. He was also a reporter for *Negro World*, and a poet. "Hit him in the mouth and push his face right in, / Knock him down a flight of stairs and pick him up again," Poston wrote in a poem called "When You Meet a Member of the Ku Klux Klan."[23]

She was admitted to the Fontainebleau School of Fine Arts in France—one of only one hundred Americans to be chosen. In April 1923, her offer of admission was rescinded after the American selection committee found out that she was black.[24] ("Her passport had been signed and other preparations for the trip had been made when two white girls reported that Miss Savage was a colored student.")[25] "I was much surprised when they told me I was a little too dark," Savage said.[26] Urged on by Du Bois, she protested publicly, especially after she was flooded with letters from people all over the country accusing her of trying to pass for white:

> They seem to have the notion that I must be a mulatto or octoroon. . . . Now I happen to be unmistakable, and that way is obviously out of the question. Isn't it rather odd that such people should always suppose that when a colored girl gets a chance to develop her natural powers it must be that she will want to be white?

"How am I to compete with other American artists if I am not given the same opportunity?" she asked.[27] A public meeting was held in May; a delegation was sent to President Harding.[28] The decision was not overturned.[29]

In June, three months after she met Gould, Savage married Robert Lincoln Poston. She was soon pregnant. Within a year of the wedding, Poston died of pneumonia while returning from Liberia, where he had attempted to arrange for the mass migration of American blacks. Savage gave birth to a daughter named Roberta; the baby died ten days later.[30]

Gould made his literary debut. In Greenwich Village, he'd met up with men he'd known at Harvard, like Cummings. Gould was drawn to Harlem, but he was always most comfortable with

Ivy League men, "old American stock." And they
liked him, too. They found him amusing, his eccen-
tricity, his hatreds, exotic. Cummings turned one
of Gould's witticisms into verse:

> as joe gould says in
>
>
> his terrifyingly hu
> man man
> ner the only reason every wo
> man
>
>
> should
> go to college is so
> that she never can (kno
> wledge is po
> wer) say o
>
>
> ifi
> 'd
> OH
> n
> lygawntueco
> llege[31]

During the war, Cummings and Slater Brown
had spent four months together in a prison in
France: Cummings had written an autobiographi-

cal novel about it, called *The Enormous Room*.[32] Brown and Malcolm Cowley were also editors of a literary magazine called *Broom* (it published Pablo Picasso, John Dos Passos, and Virginia Woolf). In October 1923 there appeared in *Broom*, in an issue containing poems by Cummings and William Carlos Williams, "Chapter CCCLXVIII of Joseph Gould's History of the Contemporary World."[33]

The title, like much of the Oral History itself, was meant satirically. People who read Gould's notebooks generally thought he was writing a parody of historical scholarship.[34] (Gould also presented himself as a fake historian. Once, asked who was his favorite historian, he said, "There's a sense of rivalry. Perhaps I don't like any. Well, I could say Beard.")[35] The chapter was introduced by a sketch of Gould drawn by Joseph Stella and a little essay, "Joseph Gould: The Man," written by Brown and Edward Nagel, Cummings's roommate. It contains the first published description of Gould's notebooks, which numbered, already, in the hundreds:

> It is this mass of grimy note-books which contain (or rather partially represent), for the fecundity of Mr. Gould passes all natural bounds, his omnivorous history of the contemporary world. Written in a cramped and curiously pedantic hand this work, which now reaches many hundred volumes, touches upon

every phase of human, animal, vegetable, and mineral activity. For Mr. Gould is restricted by no subject, neither by the limits of time or space, decency or virtue, interest or insignificance, by the air above or the waters under the earth. His only requirement to which he persistently holds is that no fact shall enter his history which he has not seen with his own eyes or heard with his own ears.[36]

Despite the fact that "Chapter CCCLXVIII of Joseph Gould's History of the Contemporary World" reads like a parody, its appearance in *Broom* earned Gould the terribly serious attention of Ezra Pound, who lived in Italy. Pound had a reputation for picking up strays.[37] Yeats wrote about him, "Sometimes about ten o'clock at night I accompany him to a street where there are hotels upon one side, upon the other palm-trees and the sea, and there, taking out of his pocket bones and pieces of meat, he begins to call the cats."[38] Gould became one of Pound's cats.

Having read the chapters of the Oral History that Gould had sent O'Brien, Pound classed him among the most distinctive and original of young American writers. (He was especially attracted to Gould's theory about hatred for blacks as against hatred for Jews.) "We have, of course, distinctly American authors, Mr Frost for example," Pound wrote. "But there is an infinite gulf between Mr

Frost on New England customs, and Mr Gould on race prejudice; Mr Frost having simply taken on, without any apparent self-questioning a definite type and set of ideas and sensibilities, known and established in his ancestral demesne. That is to say he is 'typical New England.' Gould is no less New England, but parts of his writing could have proceeded equally well from a Russian, a German, or an exceptional Frenchman."[39]

What little money Gould earned came from his work on an encyclopedia called *Who's Who in Colored America*, published by the Phillis Wheatley Publishing Company.[40] He wrote to William Carlos Williams, "They want to include all representations of African blood."[41] He was researching genealogies, tracing pedigrees.

Pound paid to have parts of Gould's Oral History typed, and began sending them to magazines.[42] Gould had found that the great work needed a series of "introductory essays," containing his thoughts on art and life.[43] "To make another human being all that is needed is a man and a woman and a spasm of lust," he wrote in an essay published in *Exile*. "To make a poem or a piece of music, you need heredity, environment and the divine gleam."[44] While Gould wrote contemptuously, about sex and birth, Augusta Savage, who had borne and lost a child, returned to her art.

·   ·   ·

In 1926 Savage went to Baltimore to exhibit twenty-two of her pieces.[45] Gould wrote her letters; she asked him to stop. Out of clay she molded the figure of a young black man looking back at the past but striding forward. After Locke, she called it *The New Negro*. "There is in New York tonight a black woman molding clay by herself in a little bare room," Du Bois wrote in 1927. "Surely there are doors she might burst through, but when God makes a sculptor, he does not always make the pushing sort of person who beats his way through doors thrust in his face."[46] Du Bois arranged for Savage to meet with a patron, who agreed to pay for a year's study at Rome's Royal Academy of Fine Arts. "We got on famously," Savage reported to Du Bois.[47] But Savage couldn't raise her share of the money she'd need to spend a year in Italy. So she stayed in New York, teaching neighborhood children to sculpt out of soap, for free.[48] She was also supporting the remains of her family: after a hurricane destroyed their house in Florida, seven members of her family, including her father, now paralyzed, moved into her tiny apartment.[49]

That tiny apartment was at the heart of the Harlem Renaissance, a gathering place for artists and for poets like Claude McCay and writers like Dorothy West.[50] "I consider you my very dearest friend," Savage wrote to the poet Countee Cullen.[51] With Langston Hughes and Zora Neale Hurston, she planned a magazine called

Fire!!. Richard Bruce Nugent described the parties she gave in a poem called "Smoke, Lilies and Jade":

> writing . . . or drawing . . . or something . . . or something about the things he felt and thought . . . then to Augusta's party . . . Langston . . . ready . . . down one hundred thirty-fifth street . . . fy-ah . . . meet these people and leave . . . fy-ah Lawd . . . now to Augusta's party . . . fy-ahs gonna burn my soul.[52]

Gould must have been at some of those parties, too. *Now to Augusta's*. He began telling people they were having an affair. She denied it. He wrote about her in his notebooks. She asked him to stop.[53] He would not.

In 1926, Gould began claiming that most of "The Oral History of Our Time" was obscene, or indiscreet, and could be published only after he was dead. "It is you know my worst handicap that much of my best material is not intended for general publication in this generation," he wrote Cummings.[54] Later, the writer Morris Werner said, "He did everything he could to avoid publication." One day, Gould stopped by Werner's apartment at 61 West 12th Street and asked him to type up some pages of the manuscript. Werner asked him if he knew any editors. "Some editors boast about knowing <u>me</u>," Gould scoffed. Werner asked about the length of the manuscript:

> He did not put it in number of words, but he went up to a 12 volume set of the Messages and Letters of the Presidents of the United States I had bought for my work. They were bulky volumes. Stretching out his dirty little hands he said: "If boiled down, it would fit this many volumes."[55]

In 1927, Pound proposed sending the Oral History to the publisher Horace Liveright. "I am not on very good terms with him," Gould answered, describing an earlier encounter: "He kept insisting that because I was intelligent I must have Jewish blood."[56] Gould always performed his anti-Semitism for the anti-Semitic Pound, telling him on one occasion that he hated "that boot licking keik Paul Rosenfeld" (Rosenfeld was a critic), and on another that he wished "the literary world were not quite as lousy with keik pants-pressers" (the poet Louis Zukofsky's father was a Yiddish-speaking pants presser).[57] Cummings tried to arrange for Simon and Schuster—he called the firm Shoeman and Scheister—to read the history. Gould one day stopped by Werner's apartment and talked to Cummings. Werner told this story:

"Gould, have you written to Simon & Schuster yet?" Cummings asked.

"No," Gould said and looked a little shame-faced. Then he asked me for a piece of my stationery. Unthinking, I gave him one with my name and address on it and he sat down and started writing.

"Are you writing to Simon & Schuster on my letter head?" I asked.

"Yes."

I took it away from him and gave him a piece of blank typewriting paper.

"I'll write to Simon & Schuster about you on my letter head, I told him, but you won't."

He started the letter, "Gentlemen, if any," and giggled. I told him sternly that it was all very funny but that if he wanted to get his ms. published it was hardly the approach, for I happened to know that there were no gentlemen at Simon & Schuster.

Gould never sent the letter.[58]

Pound warned Gould not to be so truculent. But Gould's grandiosity made any editorial conversation difficult. He challenged more than one editor to a duel. He'd write wildly outsized reviews and then abandon them if an editor wished to make cuts. "He brought me back enough manuscript to fill three complete editions of *The Sunday Tribune*," one editor said.[59] He sneered. "I do not see any point in submitting my work to your splendid mausoleum of European reputations," Gould told Marianne Moore at *The Dial*.[60] (Zukofsky and Pound had arranged for Moore to meet Gould and to read his notebooks.)[61] But after he bared his teeth at her and she didn't flinch, he was courteous with Moore, who published two essays from the Oral History.[62]

"I will have some more manuscript for you to look over," Gould wrote her. "I wish however that you could see your way to letting me do some revisions." He was picky, but in an interesting way, writing Moore, "I am anxious that the capital N in Negro be preserved as it is a pleasing courtesy to that race which resents being neglected to small letters as a kind of literary Jim Crowism."[63]

Gould respected Moore. "I am sorry that I did not have more criticism from you," he wrote her in December 1928.[64] Moore asked to see more chapters, but *The Dial* folded the next month.[65] This inspired Gould's only well-known piece of writing:

Who killed the *Dial*?
I, said Joe Gould, with my inimitable style.

One of the essays Gould published in *The Dial* is called "Marriage."[66] He asked Augusta Savage to marry him. If he wrote down her answer, he never let anyone read it.[67]

7

I have created nothing really beautiful, really lasting.

—AUGUSTA SAVAGE

She said no. He fell apart. "Augusta had flirted with me to attract someone else and I had a bad nervous breakdown," Gould explained in an essay from the Oral History called "My Life."[1] That essay, like everything else Gould ever wrote about Augusta Savage, or about the Harlem Renaissance, was never published. Much of it he may have destroyed. "I came near burning everything that I had written," he wrote in a letter to Pound, though he never told Pound about Savage.[2] "When I snapped out of it, I tried to make up for lost time. I wrote day and night." He became convinced he was going blind.[3]

I got to thinking that what had at first looked like contradictions weren't contradictions at all. Instead, they were evidence of a pattern. The Oral History existed, and then it didn't; it didn't, and then it did. He wrote it; he lost it. He was a genius; he was a blind man. Gould always said that most of his history was revision. Dwight Macdonald believed that Gould threw away the manuscript every January and began all over again, "editing, adding, deleting, and revising, lovingly distilling his information and comment into suitable form until the next revolution of the relentless year brings him to the beginning of a new version."[4] Maybe he did throw most of it away and start it again. But the parts that he kept and the parts that he destroyed were different. It's his record of her that's really missing.

I went to see the Augusta Savage Papers. They're housed in an archive on the second floor of the library on 135th Street where Savage and Gould first met in 1923. Savage once told the collector Arthur Schomburg that she wanted the world "to see Harlem through Harlem's eyes."[5] The library on 135th Street has since become the Schomburg Center for Research in Black Culture. Savage's papers consist of two slim boxes, containing mainly clippings of newspaper articles and manuscripts of children's books that Savage wrote and never published. She rarely wrote letters, and the letters she received she didn't keep. She left no diary, no real account of herself. Her legacy, she always said, was her students. "My monument will be in their work," she said.[6] Much of her own art is either lost or didn't last. She never cast most of her work; she couldn't afford bronze, or time in a foundry. She sculpted in plaster and painted it to look like bronze, using a formula she made out of shoe polish.[7] Some of her work has been stolen. Much of it, though, it appears she herself destroyed.

I went back and reread the ten volumes of Gould's diaries that I had found at New York University. Gould sometimes wrote about a "colored sculptures," but instead of writing her name, he usually left a blank space.[8] In other archives, all over the country, Gould is everywhere; Savage is hardly anywhere. The asymmetry of the written historical record was the whole reason Gould had begun the Oral History in the first place: he wanted to correct that asymmetry by writing down speech. *I imagine that the most valuable sections will be those which deal with groups that are inarticulate such as the Negro.* But in destroying the chapters of the Oral History that chronicled the Harlem Renaissance—in erasing Savage even from his diary—he'd reproduced that asymmetry. He'd made it worse. Or, no, the closer I looked, the more likely it seemed that *she'd* done it, that she'd asked him to destroy everything he'd written about her. It was very hard to know.

I tried piecing together fragments about Savage that I found here and there, colored shards of broken tile. I found a paragraph from the Oral History that sounded like a story Savage, the daughter of a firebrand preacher, might have told Gould:

A negro preacher in the south enjoyed baptizing new converts by immersion in the river. He enjoyed it most when they made a great deal of noise. One short stout woman from beyond the mountains was brought to him to be baptized. He took her out to the river and shoved her under the water.

She bobbed right up and he said, "Do you believe?"

She said nothing.

He ducked her under again and when she came up, asked her again, "Do you believe?"

She said nothing.

He pushed her under a third time and this time kept her under a while. When he let her up this time, he said, "Do you believe?"

Still the woman said nothing. He became irritated and shoved her under again and in spite of her struggling, kept her under a good time. At last he let her up. "Do you believe?" he said.

"I do," she said. He faced her towards some people on the shore and said, "Tell these people what you believe."

"I do believe this man's trying to drown me."[9]

It seemed, I thought, like a story that Savage could have told not only to Gould, but also about him, and about how she was wise to him, and wise, too, to what white modernist writers and artists were doing to the writers and artists of the Harlem Renaissance. He said he was trying to save her, but really he was trying to drown her.

It took me months to find out that Augusta Savage had been the subject of Gould's long and terrifying obsession. Nearly every trace of her was gone. I'd never have found her if it hadn't been for Millen Brand.

"Millen Brand has read a great deal of the history," Gould told Joseph Mitchell in 1942, when Mitchell was interviewing him about the Oral History for "Professor Sea Gull."[10] Mitchell set that aside: he didn't meet with Brand, or even call him; he wasn't much interested, then, in finding and reading the Oral History. But in 1964, after *The New Yorker* published "Joe Gould's Secret," Brand was among the many people who wrote to Mitchell to tell him the Oral History did exist. "Much as I hate to detract from the fine effect of your articles," he wrote, in a letter I found among Mitchell's papers, "Joe showed me long sections of the Oral History that were actually oral history."[11] These, Brand explained, "were definitely oral history as he defined it and meant it. Fragments of heard speech here and there, and the longest stretch of it, running through several composition books and much the longest thing probably that he ever wrote, was his account of Augusta Savage, the Negro sculptress."[12]

Brand knew Gould through his wife, the poet Pauline Leader, who'd met Gould in 1927.[13] Born in Vermont, Leader had lost all of her hearing when she was twelve years old. At seventeen, she ran away from home and went to New York to become a writer. "My poetry became the door that led me out of my deafness," she later wrote. She got a job as a dishwasher. At night, after her shift, she'd go to a cafeteria in Greenwich Village full of poor poets and writers. "They did not seem to mind my deafness." She couldn't hear them, but they'd write her notes. "They wrote in my cheap notebook and perhaps when someone else had the notebook and they wished to say something to me and could not wait, they used the napkins as paper."[14] It was in one of those cafeterias that Leader met Joe Gould, who wrote her notes in his dime-store notebooks. She moved into the Hotel Bradford, into a room that adjoined Gould's.[15] Three of Leader's poems appeared in *Poetry*.[16] She wrote an autobiography called *And No Birds Sing*.[17] Brand read it and wrote to her.[18] After Leader introduced Brand to Gould, he read some of the Oral History. Soon after that, Brand began writing *The Outward Room*, a novel about a patient who escapes from an insane asylum.

In the 1920s, when Brand was a student at

Columbia, he'd worked as a psychiatric aide.[19] At the time, especially at wards for the poor, the treatment was confinement itself: the relentlessly dull routine of the institution was meant to remedy the disorder of a diseased mind. Order answered chaos.[20] Brand set *The Outward Room* at Islington asylum, where Miss Cummings (a name closely associated with Gould) listens all day to the same record over and over again, "on and on, unchanging, in a continual and unchanging repetition."[21]

After *The Outward Room*, a critical sensation, Brand became a literary editor; he had an excellent editorial eye. When Brand wrote to Mitchell in 1964, he told him that he'd read about thirty-five thousand words of Gould's Oral History,[22] and that the longest and best parts of it chronicled the Harlem Renaissance; the part about Savage "was full of orality and talk and was a fairly fascinating and skillful piece of writing."[23] If those notebooks no longer existed, Brand told Mitchell, it was because Gould had probably destroyed everything he'd ever written about Savage: "It would be like him."[24]

In the summer of 1929, after Savage told Gould she didn't want to marry him, Gould fell apart, and Savage left New York for Paris. Her most accomplished work, *Gamin*, a nine-inch-high figure of a small boy from the streets of Harlem, had earned her considerable acclaim, and she'd won a fellowship from the Julius Rosenwald Fund. "I hope you will continue to work primarily with Negro models," an officer from the fund wrote to her. "I hope also you will try to develop something original, born out of a deep spirituality which you, as a Negro woman, must feel."[25] Quite what she felt she did not usually say.

"Augusta Savage is here," Countee Cullen wrote to Dorothy West in October. "She is one of my prime delights." Du Bois had arranged for Cullen to meet Savage when she reached Paris, and to introduce her to the city's writers and artists in exile. (At the time, Cullen was married to Du Bois's daughter.)[26] Savage's years in Paris were the happiest of her life, though she didn't entirely escape Gould. Cummings sought her out, with messages, when he visited France.[27] But she was freed from her domestic obligations; she had better materials and more models; and she produced a remarkable body of work in wood and marble and clay and bronze: figures of black women reclining, dancing, fighting, thinking. "It is African in feeling but modern in design," she said of her work, "but whatever else might be said it is original."[28]

Modernists sneered at realism and cultivated primitivism. (Gould liked to say that "the trobble with the bahr-bay-ree-ans is that they ol-wez bee-come civil-eyezed.")[29] But Savage rejected white artists' fetish for the primitive as African.

"I am opposed to the theories of the critics that the American Negro should produce African art," she said. And she rejected, too, the conventions of modernism.[30] "I am a realist instead of a modernist," she insisted.[31] Only four works from Savage's time in Paris have been found, but photographs of much of the lost work survive.[32] There are tributes to Haiti and allusions to Africa, and a work of clay called *Mourning Victory:* a black female figure stands, head bowed, peering down at a man's severed head, lying at her feet.[33]

By then, Gould was in the Outward Room. He never admitted to having been committed. He liked to say, "I'm my own sanitarium. I sort of carry it around with me."[34] He had certain ruses, little concealments. "I have been a very unsettled condition," he wrote to William Carlos Williams in August 1929, from a Central Islip post office box. He said that he was living on a chicken farm and would be back soon.[35] He always told Mitchell that he stored most of his notebooks on a chicken farm in Long Island. That chicken farm was a one-thousand-acre farm in Central Islip known as the Manhattan State Hospital for the Insane.[36]

8

This repetition of records was the only pleasure
she knew, to play them over and over for hours at
a time.

—MILLEN BRAND,
The Outward Room

In 1929, while he was confined at the Manhattan State Hospital for the Insane, Gould wrote a short story called "The Proud Man and the Colored Singer."[1] It's the story of a man, a not-at-all-disguised Gould, a Yankee here called Blye, who falls in love with a black artist, Savage, here not a sculptor but a singer without a name. (He always erased her name.) It begins:

God once summoned the angel who had
charge of his Department of Moral Statistics.
He said, "Invent some instrument to measure
pride. Go down to earth with it and measure

the way in which pride is distributed up in that plaguey little planet."

So the angel invented a pridometer to measure pride and after much less time than it takes a Congressional Committee to make a report he presented a summary of what he had learned. John Blye had 21% of the World's pride. Other New England Yankees had 15%. The Mandan Indians had 13%. The Kru tribe of Africa had 12%. The Asiatics had 9%. Other whites than Yankee, other Indians than Mandans, other Negroes than Krus had in their groups each 8% of the World's pride. Woodrow Wilson had 8% and the Pope had 2%.

God and the statistical angel decide to break Blye's pride by sending him a beautiful black woman to fall in love with. "He had never expected to fall in love with any woman whose ancestral bones were not mingled with those of his own progenitors in some bleak New England graveyard," Gould wrote. But "when John Blye first met the Colored Singer a most remarkable transformation came over him and in a flash all his pride disappeared. . . . He recognised that the best blood of many races blended in her and he liked the combination." To earn her love, he decides to research his own genealogy in order to prove that African blood flows in his veins. But

"Chronology seemed to interfere with the pedigree that his hypothesis demanded, so he relentlessly thrust it aside so that he might think of himself as the Negro that he wanted to be." The story ends:

> One day he encountered the Colored Singer and when she said, "You are looking darker, Mr. Blye," . . . the smile which she gave him cheered his weary soul for many a long day.[2]

It was likely at Central Islip, in 1929, that Joe Gould lost his teeth. "The first thing they did with all patients was take out all their teeth," wrote the psychiatrist Muriel Gardiner, recalling her residency at a mental hospital in New Jersey at the time. This was on the theory, she explained, "that mental illness of any sort was always the result of a physical infection."[3] It didn't help.

Still, while Savage was in Paris, Gould got back on his feet. He left the hospital, returned to the Village, and began writing the Oral History all over again. Cummings wrote Pound that Gould had recovered and was "mightily distant from a fit of the incheerfuls."[4] Malcolm Cowley hired him as a regular reviewer for *The New Republic*, where his reviews appeared alongside essays by Edmund Wilson and Lewis Mumford.[5] (The contributors' page listed him this way: "JOE GOULD, anthropologist and critic, has abandoned poetry to devote himself exclusively to his oral history of the world.")[6] "I am reviewing about fifteen books a week," Gould reported to Pound in the spring of 1930. "Of course, I am a book-reviewer not a critic. That, I fear, is a distinction. It seems marvelous how many critics they are. And the blathering pother they make. . . . Here is something cheerful to think about. To some extent the radio will supersede printing. That is good. There will be fewer books."[7] (The Oral History, he once explained, would include a discussion of this transformation: "I intend to write a series of chapters on the various means of communication, from oxcarts to airplanes.")[8]

Things didn't go well for long. "Are you plunderable?" Gould would say to men, asking for money. But "Are you gropable?" was closer to the question he asked women, especially "colored girls," except that he didn't usually ask permission. Later entries from his diary about nights at bars read like this: "I got two other women to kiss me"; "I felt some breasts"; "A girl with lovely breasts leaned over me. I kissed her several times"; "A very fresh girl was sitting at the counter. She gave a good leg show however she talked too much."[9] If he could get their addresses, he'd visit them; he'd write letters; he wouldn't leave them alone. But "when a very charming young

lady nearly sent me to jail for a letter I wrote during a nervous breakdown," he explained in "Freedom," an essay from the Oral History published
in 1931, "I did not look forward to the experience
at all."[10] He got caught.

In 1942, Horace Gregory told Mitchell something about Gould's harassment of women,
though he brushed it aside: he said that an "old
maid had him arrested," and that Gregory and
Edmund Wilson had signed statements "as character witnesses."[11] So far as I can tell, Mitchell
didn't investigate that story, or talk to any of the
women who'd filed charges against Gould (there
appear to have been at least three). Nor did he
mention any of it in print. According to Morris
Werner, Gould was arrested for assault in October 1930 and a judge was about to commit him
to an asylum when "Cummings, Edmund Wilson
and some others went down to court and heartily
perjured themselves by testifying that he was not
insane."[12] Gould was released.

One way to think about the legend of Joe
Gould, then, is that it was a fiction contrived by
men who wanted to help him stay out of an institution. They'd seen how far he'd declined at Islip:
he came back with no teeth! Beginning in 1930,
Cummings, Gregory, Wilson, and other writers
tried to protect Gould by getting him publicity. The idea seems to have been that if Gould
were better known, he could sell the Oral His-

tory and get off the streets, and either he would stop bothering women or (as would turn out to be the case) could more easily get away with it. "Some of my friends were rather worried about the threat to my liberty," Gould told Pound, "and as a result Horace Gregory placed an article on me with 'The New Republic' which will appear in the spring book number, the best possible time. He said that if I had only been sent to jail that he could have sold my book for me. That does not seem quite as nice as it might be but it is something to think over. I would not be able to write in jail so it is out of the question."[13]

Horace Gregory's loving essay, "Pepys on the Bowery," appeared in *The New Republic* in April 1931. He wrote, "The history, a library in itself, is written in longhand on the pages of fifty to a hundred high-school copy books. It is in its eighth definitive version."[14] In 1942, when Mitchell interviewed him, Gregory said that he had read at least fifty of Gould's notebooks containing, among other things, "gossip overheard in Greenwich Village and Harlem," and found them "extremely interesting," with "flashes of New England wit" and "great clarity of expression," but that it was "difficult to get editors to go through them" and much of it was unprintable "because of obscenity."[15]

Gregory's article gained Gould national attention. "No review of Greenwich Village could be complete without mentioning Joe Gould," *The Dallas Morning News* reported in September 1931:

> Gould consumes more cigarettes than any other ten men in the Western Hemisphere. He is also writing a minute survey of our times. In his room in the dilapidated Bradford Hotel are over 500 manuscript books filled with very small handwriting: this is his history. Ezra Pound published a chapter of this amazing work in his magazine, Exile. The Dial put out another chapter in the issue just before it folded up. Gould proudly claims that it was his work which caused the death of the Dial.[16]

He became a stock character: the last bohemian.

In October 1931, on the strength of his growing fame, Gould began the process of applying for a Guggenheim Fellowship.[17] He wished to study in Paris.[18] He intended to bring his mother.[19] He missed the deadline by a day.[20] When Henry Allen Moe, the head of the Guggenheim program, wrote Gould that his application would not be considered, Gould wrote back to complain that he ought to have been given a special dispensation "because of my greater need and the greater importance of my work."[21] He then began yelling at Moe in public, and later tried to apologize ("I was in a rather disturbed state of mind").[22] He applied again in 1932, when he was more desper-

ate: Cowley had by now fired him from his job at
The New Republic.[23]

Gould's falling-out with Cowley began after
Cowley reviewed a book by Melville and Frances Herskovits about "the bush Negroes of Dutch
Guiana" that Gould had wanted to review himself.[24] "Poor white trash like Cowley should get
some one to piss on him so that he at least smells
like a man before he writes about primitive people," Gould wrote to Millen Brand.[25]

After that, Cowley would still print a piece of
Gould's every once in a while. "Americans are
likely to underestimate their history, because it
all happened so rapidly," he wrote in one review.[26]
More often, he wrote doggerel:

> With his own petard
> On May the foist,
> I hope to see
> William Randolph Hoist[27]

Eventually, Cowley stopped accepting Gould's
work and just paid him, making contributions to
what came to be called "The Joe Gould Fund."[28]

Gould had asked Pound to write him a letter to
support his Guggenheim application, but Pound,
who had been in a years-long feud with Moe,
refused, telling Gould, "My name on your recommendation will indubitably prevent your getting a scholarship."[29] Gaston Lachaise wrote him

a short letter of recommendation, mentioning the work ("From time to time he would read me a chapter of his oral history, and this has always been of very great interest to me and a joy to hear English beautifully written") and commending his diligence ("Mr. Gould has carried on his work with absolute regularity for all these years with unabated enthusiasm and with a fortitude equal to the extraordinary difficulties which came before him").[30] His only other letter of recommendation came from John Olaf Evjen, a scholar of Scandinavian studies from the Augsburg Seminary in Minneapolis. In 1916, Gould had written a review of Evjen's monograph *Scandinavian Immigrants in New York, 1630–1674*.[31] He'd then gone to visit Evjen; they spent two hours together, and Evjen was so impressed that he'd asked Gould to give a lecture at the seminary and it had been a great success. Evjen had never seen him again, but remembered him vividly:

> He came into my life as a flash, a pleasing little fellow of most engaging ways, interested in a thousand things, even in the political affairs of Albania: gentle, polite, versatile, combining the traits of a historian, a sociologist and man of letters, too mindful of truth to be rubricated as a journalist, and yet possessing the qualities of one of them to a notable degree. I admired his candor.[32]

This sounds a lot like the man Joseph Mitchell met in 1942. If Gould came into your life in a flash, and left in a flash, he could be like that. *Gentle, polite, versatile, combining the traits of a historian, a sociologist and a man of letters . . .*

With his Guggenheim application, Gould submitted a list of his publications, but Moe kept asking him to submit portions of the unpublished manuscript: "Have you any item of evidence of your work which we ourselves may consider?"[33] Gould stalled: "I have had rather serious trouble with my eyes, and this has meant that it was practically impossible to prepare any of my manuscript in a legible form." He offered to meet with the judges and recite the Oral History instead.[34] Then he dodged.[35] In the end, much of his application amounted to bluster: "If the committee is intelligent enough it will judge me by two facts that are as well documented as any in current literary history. I have created a new literary form of vital interest. Competent critics believe that I have written some things that will last as long as the English language."[36]

The heart of the application was a nine-page typewritten "Synopsis of the Oral History." The book's chapters were arranged geographically, Gould explained, covering all seven lands and all four seas. "In my section on polar exploration I have much verbal information about life in the Arctic." "I have been in every province in Canada." "I have hitherto unrecorded folklore about George Washington and Thomas Jefferson." "I next take up Mexico." "I have talked with natives or visitors to every country in South America." "I begin my European section with a chapter on the Great War. I then discuss it nation by nation." "I have oral information about nearly every port of Asia. I have entertained at my home Rustum Rustomji, the Parsi; Professor Tejah Singh, a Sikh; and Lala Lajput Rai, the Hindu nationalist. My African material includes data from members of Negro tribes, as well as from Boers and explorers." He ended with more bluster: "If I receive a Guggenheim award, international and possibly interplanetary confidence in the committee will be increased."[37] It was gibberish.

Gould's application was rejected. He did, though, get a book contract, for a book to be called *Cosmopolychromatic: Selections from the Oral History.* It was to be published by his old friend Edmund Brown, or at least Gould imagined that was the case. "You will feel more confidence in my book when you see a few chapters," he wrote Brown. "If it is possible I wish you could send me some advance," he asked the next year. Then he told him, "You can make a killing on the Oral History if you handle it intelligently." When Brown asked him to submit the manuscript, Gould turned on him: "You used to have enterprise and guts. What has become of them?"

Brown wanted the manuscript typed. Gould said that was impossible. "My muscular coordination is poor. As you know I am left-handed in both hands. At the present time the nervous strain would be bad for my eyes."[38] *Cosmopolychromatic* was abandoned.

"Of course Joe Gould, he aint printed," Pound wrote to Williams. Or, as Gould put it, "Things seem to be getting wusser and wusser."[39]

9

I, too, sing America.

—LANGSTON HUGHES,
"I, Too"

Augusta Savage returned from Paris in September 1931. Straightaway, Joe Gould began threading himself into her life. "Miss Savage is giving a party," he wrote to Countee Cullen that November, "and she asked me to invite you."[1] But, later, he admitted that when Savage returned to New York she refused to speak to him.

She'd grown confident and cosmopolitan and commanding, and increasingly outspoken about art and race. "Something typical, racial, and distinctive is emerging in Negro art in America," she said.[2] She had shipped home much of her work. "I have brought back some 18 or so pieces," she reported; "some are quite large." She placed them in paid storage and worried about where to find the money to keep them.[3] She opened a school, the Savage Studio of Arts and Crafts. She was named the first director of the Harlem Community Art Center. She founded a club called the Vanguard, to talk about race and politics.[4] This attracted the attention of the FBI. For years, the bureau had spied on the leaders of the Harlem Renaissance. Now its agents began spying on Savage, too.[5] She grew bitter. She hardened.

Savage was the subject of FBI concern for more than a decade. Gould never drew the Bureau's attention.[6] Most of Savage's FBI surveillance file is redacted, pages of white covered with smears of black. On one page, the Vanguard—"An association of Negro and white intellectuals for social study and protest," with Augusta Savage as chairman—appears alongside the American Civil Liberties Union on a typewritten list headed "THE COMMUNIST PARTY: NATIONAL PROFESSIONAL ORGANIZATIONS AND ORGANIZATIONS OF PROFESSIONALS."[7]

Whoever else was following her, Gould shadowed Savage's every move. He called her; he wrote her. He berated her for betraying his secrets: "I have been told you informed people that I was in an asylum when I was in Central Islip," he wrote to her, furious. If he had lost his mind, this, he insisted, was her fault. "I have had to fight for my sanity, and some of it would have been avoided, if I could have had a real talk with you, on your first return from Europe." He said that her rejection of him was proof that she didn't really "believe in racial equality."[8]

In February 1933, Alice Neel painted a portrait of Gould, naked. Neel knew Savage. Gould asked Neel to plead with Savage on his behalf. "She and I went to call on Augusta," he wrote.[9] Savage was unmoved. Neel painted Gould sitting on a stool, his legs spread wide, his hands resting on his knees. He has three penises and three sets of testicles.[10] (Cowley said when he saw the portrait, "The trouble with you, Alice, is that you're not romantic.") "I call it 'Joe Gould,'" Neel said, "but I probably should call it, 'A Portrait of an Exhibitionist.'"[11]

In 1934, Gould began telling people that he and Savage were about to get married. "Intermarriage has tremendous difficulties, as I realize," he wrote to Pauline Leader.[12] The engagement seems to have been a figment of his imagination. Savage refused to see or speak with him. "I wrote her several letters which she did not answer," Gould admitted, and "she complained to others that I was pestering her."[13]

Savage stopped producing much new work, and what little she produced was worse than what she'd made before. She resigned from the Vanguard. She grew distant from her friends: removed, troubled, harder, and even harder.[14]

Gould told Millen Brand that he and Savage had had a misunderstanding, and asked him to intervene. "Augusta and I have never had any chance for any explanation of our difficulty," he wrote to Brand. "She has used her vivid imagination to irritate her family against me and at the same time she has gained prestige with the intelligent members of her group by publicizing my interest in her."[15] Everything Savage said about him, Gould insisted, was a lie.

Brand wanted to be helpful. "In my then young, still somewhat naïve state, I bought this story of Joe's and met Augusta and in fact liked her and was soon in a position to broach the delicate matter of her 'misunderstanding' with Joe," Brand later recounted to Joseph Mitchell. "Her face clouded up and she hesitated, but angrily she seemed to decide to tell me what was really doing." Gould hardly ever left her alone. He wrote her endless letters. He telephoned her constantly. If she gave an exhibit, he showed up. "Joe was making her life utterly miserable."[16]

There are hints, in these letters, of violence, and even of rape. "White women have had affairs with colored men, and then have accused them of rape to protect themselves, and she is doing something equally yellow," Gould complained about Savage. "I told you that Augusta would lie to you," he wrote Brand. "She tells her family that lie about my being excited by force." Savage pointed out that Gould seemed to be immune from prosecution and that his immunity had to do with his race. This maddened Gould: "I think it is cheap for Augusta to say that a colored man could not annoy a white woman as I am her." He mocked her: "It was a silly lie for Augusta to make a racial issue out of this matter because I have ties of unbreakable friendship with Harlem."[17]

Gould then told Brand he needed to speak to Savage just one more time, to interview her for the sake of finishing the chapters about Harlem in the Oral History. He begged Brand to set up a meeting. He promised he wouldn't try anything. "I ceased to love Augusta Savage some months ago," he insisted. "I do not want to urge Augusta to marry me or anything of that sort," he promised, and "if she is not willing to see me a talk with Irene will do just as well."[18] But Savage didn't want Gould near her daughter, either.

There wasn't much Savage could do: there was no particular reason to believe the police would help her and much reason to believe they wouldn't. "It was evident that as a Negro she hesitated to take court action," Brand later wrote to Mitchell. Brand wasn't altogether sure what to make of Gould's behavior: "How much of this was incipient pathology in Joe and how much plain villainy is hard to tell."[19] But Brand was unwilling to do nothing. He told Gould to leave Savage alone.

Gould then started sending letters to Brand

and his wife, "full of obscene and malicious innu-
endoes about her past life before I had known
her." He developed for Leader what Brand called
a "sick hate." "These letters were of the most
open depravity from end to end. He also began
telephoning at four o'clock in the morning, shout-
ing obscenities. There was no more of the amusing Joe, Joe the friend, Joe the confidant," Brand
explained to Mitchell, in a letter I read in Mitchell's papers at the New York Public Library. "It
was all naked malice."[20] *Portrait of a Madman.*

I figured that Brand must have saved Gould's letters as evidence. I got on a bike and rode from
42nd Street to 116th Street, to the Columbia
University Library. There, in an uncataloged box
of Brand's papers, I found a thick folder marked
with a note: "Not to be released for use until my
death."[21]

Inside the folder were four chapters of Gould's
Oral History, together with a clutch of terrible
letters. "If I prefer to woo an American woman to
a greasy neurotic Jewess with breath stinking of
herring," Gould wrote to Leader, "do I have to ask
your approval?" After Brand told Gould to leave
Savage alone, Gould called Leader "filthier than
any prostitute" and Brand a "pimp for her intellectual whoredom." He insisted he didn't want
Savage anymore: "I would prefer not to marry her

because she is sterile and ... I could not adjust myself to going childless to the grave."[22]

Brand never mentioned this to Mitchell, but Gould hadn't only sent obscene, threatening letters to Brand and Leader; he had sent them to their son, Jonathan, a very little boy: "I realize that your father is quite naturally ashamed of the cheap tactics he is using," Gould wrote to Jonathan Brand, "but if he has intelligence enough he will realize that it would be advisable for him to have a personal talk with me before he takes legal action."[23]

Brand saw a side of Gould he had never seen before. He went to the police and got a summons for Gould's arrest—"I was not a Negro woman, and I wasn't taking it"—but Gould begged him to drop the charges, "saying he had already been taken to court on a similar charge and had received a suspended sentence, but if I went through with this, he would certainly be put in jail and he needed careful treatment of his eyes and would probably go blind."[24]

Brand arranged to meet with Gould under the arch in Washington Square. "I told him I would discontinue the action on condition that he never saw me or spoke to me or Pauline again in his life and stopped all his persecution of Augusta," Brand told Mitchell. "He agreed and that was the last I ever saw or heard from him."[25] But for Savage, the end had not come.

. . .

In 1934, Gould applied for a Guggenheim again, this time with a letter of recommendation from Edward J. O'Brien. O'Brien had read parts of the Oral History decades earlier. "To the best of my knowledge he has devoted his life to it against extraordinary conditions of want and poverty," O'Brien wrote. He considered Gould to be brilliant. More he could not say. Instead, having known Gould so long, he recommended caution. "If a very large body of material is now available I suggest that the Guggenheim Foundation might experimentally subsidise the editing and typing of a portion of it in order that it may be examined closely. . . . I am not able to judge fairly as to the final value of what he has done without having more evidence to go on."[26]

Gould's application was again rejected. He began sending Moe vicious letters, asking him personally for money and then demanding it. For a while, Moe gave him ten or fifteen dollars, but at a time when he was giving money to refugees from Europe, he wrote a note to himself, "This is the end." Gould then sent him a letter that's a good illustration of his malice:

Inasmuch as I have created a vital new literary form and have written some things which will last as long as the English language, I cannot expect as much courtesy from you as if I were a plagiarist, and since I am handicapped by being of old American stock, I realize that a foundation as yours is predisposed in favor of the predatory type of recent coolie immigrant such as the original Guggenheim.[27]

By now, hardly anyone could fail to see, he was mean; he was vicious. He was wretched and abandoned. He smelled; he was covered with sores and infested with bedbugs. He was terribly, terribly ill. Cummings made him sit on the windowsill so he wouldn't leave lice on the furniture. People would spray the room with a DDT gun as soon as he left.[28] "Quick, Henry, the Flit," the artist Erika Feist would holler to her husband when she saw Joe Gould coming up the stairs.[29]

I'd trudge, weary, to this library or that, to photograph more of Gould's letters, and I'd imagine my camera was a Flit gun. I began to think, *Joe Gould is contagious.*

Gould didn't come to Joseph Mitchell's attention by happenstance. In 1934, Edward J. O'Brien visited New York and told Gould that he ought to get himself profiled in *The New Yorker*.[30] *The New Yorker*'s interest in Gould was a product of the years-long campaign waged by Gould's friends to keep him out of an institution. "GING to git you to git some of JOE's oral HISTORY fer Esquire," Pound wrote Cummings.[31] (*Esquire* didn't print it.)[32]

Gould lost his teeth, the fakes. Cummings's sister, who was a social worker, said that if Gould went on relief, he'd get five dollars a week, and could get a pair of someone else's teeth. Gould told Cummings there were only two kinds of people on the dole: "the kind of people you wouldn't be found dead with and the kind of people who need it so much more than we do."[33] Then he began harassing Cummings's sister with unwanted letters and phone calls.[34] Meanwhile, his rent was so overdue that his landlady threw him out, and threw away all of his notebooks, too.[35] He used his food checks to buy new notebooks.[36] He got new teeth.

Millen Brand never spoke to Joe Gould again, but he sat for a bust by Augusta Savage. It took eighteen sittings, and when Savage cast the head in plaster, the ears broke off. " 'You'll have to start all over again,' she said, joking," Brand wrote in his diary. (Brand's diary is full of speech and sound; he wrote it for his deaf wife, so that she could hear his days.) He went back one evening for Savage to build up the ears. He loved sitting in her studio, watching her:

> She mixed plaster in a glass and worked quickly, adding the plaster bit by bit and shap-

ing it. She used a steel chisel. The radio in the next room had on a horror story. Fragments came through the French doors—'He is sleeping.' A scream. 'He's dead!'

"My mother listens to them all the time," Augusta said. "She likes only the stories."

Brand sat and listened. "The voices from the radio came through the quiet air: tense voices, screams, the expected deception, the bafflement, the forewarning that had no relation to us or to the peace of the night."[37] He loved the sound, and the silence.

In 1935, Gould got a job with the Federal Writers' Project. He said that he was writing a biographical dictionary of New York's earliest settlers and that he was doing it alone because he was a better writer than everyone else. "I'm a one-man project," he told the *Herald Tribune*.[38] "My own book is too good, of course," he said, "to be subsidized by a mere government."[39]

By then, Savage was the most influential artist in Harlem, not for the work she produced but for her teaching, and for the opportunities she tried to provide for younger artists. She was assistant director of the Federal Arts Project. She helped to found the Harlem Artists Guild. She organized an exhibit called *Artists and Models* at the 135th Street branch of the public library.[40]

In 1937, Savage received her most important

commission: the organizers of the 1939 World's Fair charged her with creating "a group which will symbolize the Negro's contribution to the music of the world."[41] This got her picture into *Life* magazine, illustrating a story titled "Negroes: Their Artists Are Gaining in Skill and Recognition."[42] It also led to her leaving her post as the head of the Harlem Community Arts Center—her friend Gwendolyn Bennett took over, an arrangement Savage believed to be temporary—but when Savage finished the World's Fair sculpture, she found she'd lost her job.[43]

Gould lost his job, too. He was fired. Cummings tried to intervene, writing to the head of Federal Writers' Project, Henry Alsberg. "I know Gould is an 'Institution,'" Alsberg wrote back, "but couldn't do anything to save him."[44]

And still writers loved to write about him, the writer who could not stop writing. He took to saying, "I make good copy."[45]

10

YOU might write a nize lil piece say harft a page
    about Joe's ORAL hizzery
And mebbe that wd/ start somfink IF you
    make it clear and EGGs plain WHY Joe
    izza hiz
Torian

—EZRA POUND TO E. E. CUMMINGS

In 1939, Augusta Savage held her first one-woman show, at the Argent Galleries on West 57th Street. "I have long felt that Negro artists, in the course of our development, have reached the point where they should have a gallery of their own, one devoted to the exhibition and sale of Negro art," she said.[1] She opened the Salon of Contemporary Negro Art, the United States' first ever gallery of African American art, at 143 West 125th Street. She ran a workshop called the Uptown Art Laboratory.[2] She began planning a tour of Negro colleges and universities, carrying "a small exhibition of my own and other artists' work": "Our painting and sculpture, unlike our literature and music, has too long been the property of New York, and I feel it is time for the rest of the country to know what the artists of our race are achieving."[3] And she finished her commission for the World's Fair, a sixteen-foot sculpture inspired by James Weldon Johnson's "Lift Every Voice and Sing," the so-called Negro National Anthem. "Lift every voice and sing / Till earth and heaven ring." But when the fair closed, she had no money to store that sculpture: it was demolished by a bulldozer.[4]

In 1939, Ezra Pound toured the United States.[5] He had become a Fascist and had the idea that he could help keep the United States out of war with Italy by making an argument about history, which was that democracy was impossible since the world was secretly run by Jews. "The COUNTRY needs (hell yes) an historian," he wrote Cummings.[6]

After Pound went back to Italy, where he wrote anti-Semitic essays for Italian newspapers and took to signing letters "Heil Hitler," he and Cummings redoubled their efforts to get the Oral History published. "Have done what less I could to more your most generosity around little joe," Cummings wrote Pound early in 1940, telling him that he had set up meetings for Gould. "Coached Joe, which expressed willingness sans astonishment con skepticism."[7] It was likely

through their efforts that in 1941, William Saroyan published an essay called "How I Met Joe
Gould": "Joe Gould remains one of the few genu-
ine and original and American writers," Saroyan
said, in a tribute that sums up exactly what modernists saw in Gould:

> He was easy and uncluttered, and almost all
> other American writing was uneasy and a lit-
> tle sickly; it was literary; and it couldn't say
> anything simply. All other American writing
> was trying to get into one form or another,
> and no writer except Joe Gould seemed to
> have imagination enough to understand that
> if the worst came to the worst you didn't
> need to have any form at all. You didn't need
> to put what you had to say into a poem, an
> essay, a story or a novel. All you had to do was
> say it.[8]

Pound had something to say, too. In addresses
for Radio Rome, he began attacking the United
States and the United Kingdom, which by the
end of 1941 were at war with Italy. "You let in
the Jew and the Jew rotted your empire, and you
yourselves out-jewed the Jew," Pound said on Italian radio in March 1942. "And the big Jew has
rotted EVERY nation he has wormed into."[9]

Mitchell began interviewing Gould that June.[10]
In July, Cummings rambled about the mysterious

whereabouts of Gould's history, within the Enormous Room:

> There exist secret passages among those closets or better interstices; and surely the former will end with a furlined trapdoor which (being lifted) reveals a colossal green candybox which (being opened) reveals a microscopic mahogany rolltopdesk which (via dynamite) reveals a lifestatured nugget of thoroughly once chewinggum containing at its very most exact centre Joe ("Are You Plunderable?") Gould Inc disguised as a Moslem pianotuner.[11]

"Within the year there will be a profile of me printed in the New Yorker which ought to set me up again as a reviewer," Gould reported to William Carlos Williams in October.[12] He told Lewis Mumford that he expected the profile to earn him contracts for four books.[13]

"Professor Sea Gull" appeared in *The New Yorker* in December 1942. "Joe Gould is a blithe and emaciated little man who has been a notable in the cafeterias, diners, barrooms, and dumps of Greenwich Village for a quarter of a century," the piece begins.[14] It is immensely charming and, in it, so is Gould—a delightful eccentric, a strange and wonderful little man, wandering the streets, harmlessly, in a world at war.

"The article was about ten per cent accurate,

but it has established me along with the Empire State building as one of the sights of the town," Gould wrote to Mumford when the profile appeared on newsstands. "Furthermore a couple of publishers seem to be interested in me."[15] But the interest of publishers in a book he had written and also failed to write was not something a man in severe decline could easily take. On January 13, 1943, he wrote in his diary, "I ate at the Brown's."[16] And then: he disappeared.

Slater Brown lived at Patchin Place, two floors above Cummings. For months, Brown and his wife had been feeding Gould dinner every night except Saturday. ("Joe Gould rules their roost," Cummings wrote to his sister.)[17] After that last dinner, on January 13, it took Brown four months to find Gould. When he did, he wrote to Mitchell to say that "Professor Sea Gull" was "one of the best Profiles which the New Yorker has published for years, particularly as you were not afraid to use your imagination about the Little Gentleman." But he wrote, mainly, to tell him what had happened.[18]

Right after the piece came out, Gould had gotten so drunk—he was a celebrity! he was a genius! he was the most brilliant historian of the twentieth century! he was the subject of an adoring profile in *The New Yorker*!—that he'd fallen down the stairs of the Vanguard Tavern in the Village. The evening of January 13, he had been dizzy at dinner at the Browns'. Later that night, Rex Hunter, a writer for the *Sun* who also lived at Patchin Place, found Gould lying in a pool of blood in the street, reading a chapter of the Oral History to a policeman. (Cummings told this story slightly differently; he said that Hunter had found Gould "all bloody & partially smothered in notebooks," and that "a cop, while awaiting the Saint Vincent's ambulance, attempted to read one; & failed.")[19] He'd been taken to St. Vincent's and released, but when he failed to appear at the Browns' for dinner for weeks—he must have been wandering the city, completely disoriented, because he didn't write any entries in his diaries all this time—Brown called Bellevue, on a hunch that he might have been taken in, so concussed and psychotic that he had been unable to identify himself, which was exactly what had happened. Cummings then arranged for a psychiatrist to see him; the psychiatrist, according to Brown, said "that Joe was not insane but just eccentric," though he nevertheless committed him to Wards Island, "so that he could get three meals a day, a bed, and some feeling of security."[20]

"Dear Mr. Mitchell," Gould wrote on April 3, 1943. "I am now at the Manhattan State Hospital." He was writing from Keener 6, the mental ward. "I can be visited Wednesdays, Saturdays, and Sundays, from 1 to 3 PM." He asked Mitchell to send him a copy of "Professor Sea Gull," as there was very little to read in the hospital library.[21] He hoped Mitchell might consider revising it. "It was a splendid article but it was more historical than factual."[22] (This was a joke of Gould's. History, he liked to say, was fiction.)

Mitchell went to visit him. Before, he'd seen one Joe Gould. At Manhattan State Hospital, he saw another:

> They had cut his hair and shaved off most of his beard, leaving him a clipped mustache and a Van Dyke. He said they have changed him in appearance from Trotsky to Lenin. Brought him a carton of Pall Malls, and he called another patient over and gave him a pack. In return, the other patient gave him half a candy bar. Had made a number of friends. Had composed a yell.
>
> Keener, Keener
> Sis boom bah
> Nuts to you
> Bim boom bah
>
> Had invented a game called Ward's Island polo, in which small patients, riding on the backs of large patients, knocked a rubber ball up and down the corridor using brooms for mallets.
> Said he had been confused at Bellevue.

"I saw the water from the window, the East River," he said, "and I thought I was in Martha's Vineyard, and I began to talk about Martha's Vineyard, and they decided I was crazy."[23]

The psychiatrist Mitchell talked to in Keener 6 did not believe Gould was a kindly eccentric. He believed he was a psychopath.[24]

By summer, Gould was back on the streets, albeit under the monitoring of social services. Slater Brown arranged for Max Perkins at Scribner's to read some of the notebooks. Gould wrote Mitchell, "I believe there is a fifty-fifty chance of Scribners taking my book. I hope so. They are a good firm and deserve a break."[25]

He then began once again hounding everyone he knew, every day, for cash. "Joe Gould's still out of the booby hatch, looking like something the cat brought in but 'worse and more of it,'" Cummings wrote to his sister.[26] *Wusser and wusser.*

When Gould wasn't writing, he was drinking; when he wasn't drinking, he was plundering; and when he wasn't plundering, he was groping. He could hardly have been more different from the character described in *The New Yorker.* Meanwhile, "Professor Sea Gull" lived on and Gould collected his press clippings. By July 1943, *Time* had written about him and Mitchell's profile had been reprinted in *McSorley's Wonderful Saloon*, a collection of Mitchell's essays.[27] Gould's daily rounds now included not only the offices of *The New Republic*, where Cowley was usually good for a dollar, and of the *Herald Tribune*, where Gould put the touch on editor Robert J. Cole, but also the offices of *The New Yorker* and of Scribner's. A typical day:

I got up at one. Bugs bothered me. I asked Mr. Cole for a dime for a drink. He gave me a quarter. I went to the White Rose. I had an ale. One of the bartenders came over to talk to me. He was nice. I told him I would be more sociable another time. I went back and used the Flit. The bugs still persisted. I got up late. I had coffee on my way uptown. I went to the New Republic. I had a wait for Malcolm. I had a copy of Time with my photo in it. I slept while I waited. At last Malcolm came. He gave me one half a dollar and six cents for stamps. He had a book for me. I went to Scribners. I had a long wait. I was told Mr. Perkins was very busy. At quarter of five I decided to leave. I showed Time to his secretary. She said she would tell him about it. She asked me to come in on Friday. I posted my letters at the Post Office. 25 W. 43d St. I phoned Joe Mitchell. He said to come up. I did so. He had a copy of his book for me. We chatted. I asked him if he had any clippings. He said his publisher had. The only copy I had not heard about was a mention in Newsweek which he thought mentioned me. He gave me a dollar.[28]

With Perkins, Gould performed a disordered parody of the strange arrangement that is publishing: the selling of a book to an editor, every man his manuscript. "He had typed three chapters of the Book," Gould wrote in his diary on July 30, 1943, after seeing Perkins. "He liked it very much." They'd go on like this, having an editorial chat:

> He was still puzzled by the problem of the unity of the book. I said that would clear up as I handed him more material. I also said that I was working on chapters that will not be immediately available, but that any other way of work would spoil the spirit of my history. I read him three short chapters on George II.

And then, as Perkins would do every time Gould came to visit, he would buy the book:

> He gave me a dollar. He said Friday was the best time to look in. He gave me a dollar. I got cigarettes. I had an ale in the Minetta Tavern.[29]

This went on and on. August 6, 1943: "I went to Scribners. I had a short wait for Perkins. He liked the new chapters. He gave them back typed. He gave me two dollars." August 9: "I gave him two chapters. . . . He gave me a dollar." Then Gould dropped the pretense. August 24: "I went to Scribners. Max Perkins gave me a dollar. I had no manuscript for him."[30]

Slater Brown took Gould away for a rest, to spend a few weeks with him at his house in Truro. "I have been on Cape Cod for nearly a month and have added a great deal to the oral history as well as gotten much new material," Gould reported to Mitchell that fall.[31] Brown later said that while Gould was up in Truro "he read an essay he had just written for the Oral History, read it aloud, but the strange thing was, I had heard him read the same essay a long time ago, years and years ago."[32] On the Cape, Brown composed a parody of the Oral History—"Page 3,769,300 . . . Chapter 5,768"—and sent it to Cummings. It involves a young Gould leading a girl off into the woods and asking her if she would like to see a big wolf. "She would say yes and then I would show her a wolf."[33] The wolf, of course, was Gould himself.

When Gould got back to New York, Perkins cut him off. This put more pressure on everyone else he ordinarily tapped. "I went to 597 Fifth Avenue," he wrote in his diary. "I could not see

Perkins. I phoned Joe Mitchell. He gave me two dollars." (Gould, predictably, turned on Perkins, writing to Mumford, "He is not enough of a scholar to read his own language.")[34] That wolf, he kept on showing people that wolf. "Met Joe Mitchell and his wife," Gould wrote in his diary one day. They were having drinks; he joined them. "His wife accused me of goosing her."[35]

Two undergraduates, reporters for *The Harvard Crimson* who'd read "Professor Sea Gull," went to New York to interview Gould. "They seemed naïve," Gould wrote in his diary.[36] They weren't so very naïve. "One of these days, someone is going to write an article on Joseph Ferdinand Gould '11 for the Reader's Digest," they wrote in the *Crimson*. "It will be entitled 'The Most Unforgettable Character I Have Met' and it will present Joe Gould as an unusual but lovable old man. Joe Gould is not a lovable old man."[37]

After *The New Yorker* printed "Professor Sea Gull" and readers told Joseph Mitchell that it was the best story ever written and Joe Gould became as famous as the Empire State Building, Augusta Savage left New York City. She abandoned her friends and her studio and her school, and moved to the small town of Saugerties, New York, a town whose black community had lived, for a century, on Nigger Road. She told a minister in Saugerties that she'd left New York to escape the pressure to become a recruiter for the Communist Party.[38] Millen Brand heard a rumor that she'd become an informant for the FBI. "Heard Augusta betrayed some people on the art project in Harlem," Brand wrote in his diary. "Regretted it."[39] I don't know if he meant that he regretted it or that she did. For a long time, I had a hard time believing it. I'd thought that Savage left New York only to get away from Joe Gould. But—and here's the trouble—from the moment I first learned about her, I knew that my likeliest error would be in thinking I understood Augusta Savage, as if she were me, when, really, I hardly know her at all. The error was mine: the rumor was true.[40]

In Saugerties, she moved into a house on a small farm owned by the commissioner of public welfare. The house had no electricity. It had no plumbing. She used kerosene for light and wood for heat. She scratched together a hard-scrabble living; she raised pigeons, and grew flowers, and mulled wine. Most of all, she raised chickens. It has taken me a very long time, my whole life, to learn that the asymmetry of the historical record isn't always a consequence of people being silenced against their will. Some people don't want to be remembered, or heard, or saved. They want to be left alone.

People in Saugerties told me she'd chosen their town to move to because the little boy in Harlem who'd been the subject of *Gamin* was from their town, and his family lived there.[41] Maybe it was his family that arranged for her to move into the Welfare Department's bare little house, on the side of a hill.

She took a job working at a research laboratory, taking care of the mice. The man who owned the laboratory built her a studio on that hill, and provided her with clay, year after year, so that she could still make art. A man who'd grown up next door told me he met Savage when he was five years old and that she taught him to fish. She'd cut down a cane, and tie a line, and they'd sit down at the beaver brook. When she got too old to fish, he'd go fishing and bring her his catch. A woman who lived across the street told me that friends of Savage's would take the bus up from New York, from Harlem, to visit. Late at night, in summer, Savage's neighbors would sit on their front porches to listen to the sounds coming from Savage's front porch. Their talk was like music. Their laughter was like fireworks.

◀ PART THREE ▶

Case No. 231

11

Our records from so many sources, thorough, detailed, profound, make it possible for the lay person as well as the scientist to judge the extent to which psychoanalysis can help the seriously disturbed person.

—MURIEL GARDINER,
"The Wolf-Man"

In February 1943, while Joe Gould was playing polo in Keener 6, an FBI agent knocked on E. E. Cummings's door. "Apparently someone has to identify a certain 'seditious' radio 'voice,' broadcasting shortwaveishly from Italia, as EP's," Cummings wrote to his sister. The U.S. Foreign Broadcast Monitoring Service, headquartered at Princeton, New Jersey, had been listening in on Radio Rome since 1942. (Princeton was a center for the study of radio. The Radio Research Project, launched there in 1937, is why Orson Welles's 1939 *War of the Worlds* broadcast is set in Princeton.) "I said I'd do my best if necessary but hoped I wouldn't have to," Cummings reported to his sister, although he told the FBI that he himself didn't have a radio, and wouldn't recognize even his own voice, no less Pound's. He also suggested that the FBI ask William Carlos Williams to do it instead; Williams, he thought, would be a "proper Judas."[1] Someone did it. In July 1943, Ezra Pound was charged with treason in absentia.

Gould, who once wrote an essay titled "Why Princeton Should Be Abolished," felt that he understood Pound.[2] "I will always feel some gratitude toward him although I disagree with him completely," he wrote Williams. "I felt that he was obsessed to a degree beyond mental health. This was because he seemed to be obsessed with ideas that were not in character nor consistent with the man as I had pictured him. I know of many acts of kindness on his part to Jewish people. I therefore felt that he was off balance apart from his usual enthusiastic tendency to ride any hobby of the moment too hard. In other words I thought that at that time he was temporarily haywire. I believe he would have snapped out of it if the course of events had been different."[3] *Because he is me.*

After Augusta Savage left New York, after Max Perkins cut him off, Gould staggered through the city, sicker and sicker. "I went to the clinic of Saint Vincents," he wrote in his diary on February 22, 1944. "I had to pay a dollar fee. I had a brief examination." Two days later: "Felt poorly.

Went over to Rutherford, New Jersey." (He went to Rutherford to see Williams, who was a physician.) February 24: "Oh hell." February 29: "Augusta Savage's birthday."[4] Leap year's day: her birthday came only once every four years.

On March 4, 1944, Gould heard about a woman, "a wealthy refugee doctor, who loved to shell out," who might be able to be convinced to pay his rent. "She thought she could publish my book."[5] Her one stipulation was that Gould was never to know her name. Two weeks later, urged on by his friend John Rothschild and Rothschild's wife, the artist Erika Feist, Gould went into the hospital, voluntarily.[6] He had surgery on his bladder and stayed for a month. He wrote to Joseph Mitchell, "In some ways this place reminds me of Sing Sing from which, as you may remember, I was expelled for playing too rough in the polo game against Princeton."[7]

On April 13, 1944, Gould wrote in his diary about seeing a "Doctor Gardner," a female doctor.[8] He had more appointments with her after he was discharged. The last time he went to see her was April 28.[9] On May 6, John Rothschild explained to Gould that he'd made an arrangement for him to be supported by an anonymous patroness:

> I have a wealthy friend who knows about you and your work and who is considering subsi-

dizing you for a while to the extent of providing board, lodging, and possibly laundry. The
idea is to provide you with the bare essentials
of healthy living so that you have a chance
to bring your work to fruition. You will not
receive cash; the bills will be paid for you. . . .
You will be under no obligation whatsoever.
In fact, the lady bountiful prefers to remain
anonymous.[10]

When Gould got out of the hospital, his rent,
at a place called Maison Gerard, was paid by this
mysterious benefactor. He was desperate to discover her identity. He heard her last name began
with "G." For a while, he thought she was a Guggenheim. (He was wrong.) He kept sleuthing. It
was a point of pride with Gould that no one could
evade him for long. Joseph Mitchell once tried
to get away from him by leaving the city without giving a forwarding address. Gould tried very
hard to track him down. One day, he cornered
the photographer Aaron Siskind. "He said he had
seen Joe Mitchell, who was at work on a book.
I said I will not ask his address as he seemed to
want to keep it a military secret." But, of course,
he did more than ask; he demanded.[11]

The person he was really looking for was the
person he'd been hounding since 1923. No matter
what he'd promised Millen Brand in 1934, or what
he'd promised anyone since, or how often, or how

tearfully, he never, ever left her alone. "Went to the Waldorf," he wrote in his diary early in 1945. "Had a long talk with Bruce Nugent. He promised to get me Augusta's address."[12]

The name of Gould's benefactor was Muriel Gardiner. She was a psychiatrist and psychoanalyst.[13] I am pretty certain she was the "Doctor Gardner" who examined him in the hospital. And I'm pretty sure, too, that her interest in him was clinical as much as philanthropic.

Muriel Morris was born in Chicago in 1901; her grandfather, a German Jew, had emigrated to the United States. She was the very wealthy heir of a meatpacking firm, Morris & Company. She went to Wellesley and then to Oxford, where she wrote a thesis about Mary Shelley's *Frankenstein*. She was briefly married to a man named Gardiner. Then she went to Vienna, to be analyzed by Freud, but was instead handed over to Freud's disciple, Ruth Mack Brunswick. Between 1910 and 1914, Freud had treated a Russian aristocrat named Sergei Pankejeff, who was three years older than Joseph Gould. (Freud referred to Pankejeff as the Wolf-Man, because of his childhood fear of wolves.) Freud's study of Pankejeff appeared in 1914 as "From the History of an Infantile Neurosis." Gardiner met Pankejeff in Vienna in 1926; he taught her Russian. While Brunswick was analyzing Gardiner, she was also analyzing Pankejeff. (Brunswick's "A Supplement to Freud's 'History of an Infantile Neurosis'" appeared in 1928.) In 1926 and 1927, Gardiner lived in Greenwich Village. She might possibly have met Gould at that time; her closest friend was a sculptor, who may have known Augusta Savage.[14] Returning to Austria in 1931, she trained as an analyst and went to medical school at the University of Vienna. During the 1930s she worked underground for the resistance, securing false passports to help Jewish families escape from Germany and Austria. (She also hid Joseph Buttinger, the head of Austria's socialist underground, whom she later married.) In 1938, she managed to get Pankejeff out of Vienna and into the United States. Nearly all the analysts had fled Austria, and Gardiner believed Pankejeff urgently needed analysis: "he was as much in danger of destruction from within as were my Jewish friends from Nazi brutality at the concentration camps." She and Buttinger moved to the United States in 1941. They set up a foundation, the New Land Foundation: Gardiner wanted to give away her money.[15] Buttinger headed an international aid organization, and Gardiner began a psychiatric internship in New Jersey.[16] She went by Muriel Buttinger socially but Muriel Gardiner professionally. She was zealous about her privacy.[17]

In the 1940s, during the years when Muriel

Gardiner was supporting Joe Gould, she was also
translating a memoir written by Sergei Pankejeff.
Very likely, Gardiner read "Professor Sea Gull"
in 1942 or 1943. At the time, although she lived in
New Jersey, she kept an apartment in New York.[18]
She was close to both John Rothschild and Erika
Feist. (Gardiner was a patron of Feist's work.
"Dr. Buttinger has my work all over the house,"
Feist said.)[19] It's not impossible that Gardiner also
met Gould while treating psychiatric patients.[20]
Gould often took the train to New Jersey when
he was ill; he saw Williams there, and got medicine from him. In New Jersey, Gardiner found
the care of patients in the state mental hospital
appalling. What most distressed her was the
removal of their teeth. "I read their charts," she
later said, "and some of them literally had had
teeth, tonsils, appendix, uterus, every organ that
you could live without removed for no apparent
reason except because they were schizophrenic."
Did they get well? she was asked. No, she said.
"None of them ever had got better."[21]

Gardiner supported hundreds of people, nearly
always anonymously. She was a great patron of
the arts. She also supported, for instance, Alice
Neel.[22] But Gould was more like her patients than
like the artists whose work she supported. If she
hadn't met Gould in a hospital, she'd certainly
met a great number of patients like him: declin-
ing, decaying, abandoned, toothless. She'd always

been drawn to the hardest patients. "I was interested particularly in the very difficult patients who I had been wisely advised not to take, but I took them anyhow," she said. "I was terribly interested, though they were terribly difficult."[23] Gardiner later explained why she'd agreed to support Gould: "There is a type of alcoholic or psychopath who can go ahead and accomplish something if he has a little security."[24] Also, she knew how much painting had meant to Pankejeff, how it held him together.[25] She cared about art. She wanted to rescue people, especially artists and writers. She wanted to save him.

Ezra Pound was arrested in Italy on May 8, 1945. Interviewed by an American reporter, he compared Hitler to Joan of Arc. He was jailed in an iron cage. On May 22, in Greenwich Village, Joe Gould began begging on behalf of Pound's defense.[26] On June 4, he wrote to Dwight Macdonald at *Politics:*

> Once lost now found
> Poor Ezra Pound
> Is not a hound.
> His mind's unsound.

"You may print it if you wish."[27]
He began writing to everyone he could think

of, asking for money for Pound's defense. "I want to write at least a hundred letters," he told James Laughlin, the editor of New Directions.[28] He needed only money for postage. "I am beginning to be in good shape again and am being moderately guggenheimed to the extent of fifteen dollars a week," he wrote Malcolm Cowley. "That keeps me going but is not enough to conduct as good a campaign for Ezra as I would like. If you feel that you can contribute a bit, I would appreciate it. I believe that a poet has as much right to be a damn fool as anyone else."[29]

In Pisa, Pound was examined by a team of psychiatrists, who found him mentally unstable. In November 1945, he was remanded to the United States and was committed to an insane asylum in Washington, D.C.

Apparently, Pound's confinement did not diminish his interest in getting Joe Gould's Oral History published. He and Gould corresponded. "I believe that Ezra Pound is doing all right," Gould reported to Williams in October 1946. "He gets plenty of books and has occasional visitors."[30] The next month, Pound wrote Cummings, "Joe G. still alive—have we between us force to git him printed?"[31]

While Gardiner paid his rent, Gould put on weight. "Joe Gould now looks like a moderately sized Santa Claus," Cummings wrote to his sister, "having been anonymously endowed per a female refugee."[32] He had a roof over his head, and three meals a day. Still, he spent most of his time drinking and begging, saying he was raising money for Ezra Pound.

Then, suddenly, in October 1947, Gardiner informed Feist and Rothschild that she'd decided to cut Gould off at the end of the year. Cummings wondered why. "Parait que his erstwhile refugee-backess decided she'd put her dollars on the foreign poor, pourchanger perhaps," he wrote Pound. "Or maybe Gould got fresh?"[33]

Mitchell wondered, too. When he was researching "Joe Gould's Secret," he found out that Gardiner had been Gould's patroness. She agreed to speak with him on condition that Mitchell never reveal her name. She told him that she'd never talked to Gould and didn't think she'd ever seen him. "I have a vague feeling that he was once pointed out to me in a restaurant in the Village," she said, "but I'm not sure."[34]

I suspect Gardiner might have decided not to tell Mitchell what she knew about Gould. Strong evidence suggests as much. Feist told Mitchell that Gardiner knew a lot about Gould and that "she stopped giving Joe money because he didn't do anything with himself."[35] And another Villager told Mitchell that "somebody who knew the dr ran across Gould in the Village, maybe at a party, maybe in a restaurant, and listened to him, and he or she told the dr: you're wasting your money on Joe Gould, he's not producing anything, he's not even trying." Or "maybe the dr saw him herself."[36] If Gardiner saw Gould, it would have been difficult not to notice that he was spending his time, and her money, to defend Ezra Pound.

Rothschild asked her to reconsider: "If you did read Professor Sea Gull, then you know why people love Joe Gould and want to see him continue to live, and why he has to be taken care of if he is going to survive." He begged her. "He is growing old and would not survive long. And his misery would be unbearable to behold."[37] Gardiner refused to reconsider. The money ran out in December 1947.

"The Oral History of Our Time" was never published. But it did start a movement.

"We began with paper, pen, and pencil, nothing else," the Columbia University historian Allan Nevins wrote about founding the Oral History Project in 1948. "We were therefore very thankful when, in a few years, the tape recorder came in."[38]

Gould was the first person to talk about recorded speech as oral history. "As for the term oral history, it appears to have been coined by a dissolute member of the Greenwich Village literati named Joe Gould," a director of Columbia's Oral History Research Center later admitted, with some embarrassment, adding, "The term may have slipped into Allan Nevins' vocabulary through the *New Yorker*, but his own thoughts about an ongoing interviewing effort for the benefit of future scholars germinated as far back as 1931."[39] Nineteen thirty-one, the year Nevins got the idea for the Oral History Project, is the year that Gould wrote to eminent historians all over the country telling them about "The Oral History of Our Time." Chances are he wrote to Nevins, and gave him the idea. "Apart from literary merit it will have future value as a storehouse of information," Gould wrote then. "It seems to me that the average person is just as much history as the ruler or celebrity."[40] Nevins, though, wasn't interested in the inarticulate; he was interested in rulers and celebrities.[41]

Nevins's project was extraordinarily successful. "Oral history offices were established in Wisconsin, in Massachusetts, in California, and in other parts of the Union," Nevins later recalled. "Some even appeared in foreign lands." In 1966, Nevins founded the Oral History Association (Gould had founded an organization of the same name in 1929). "Nobody has ever doubted the Oral History Office is and will continue to be invaluable to the historians of the United States," Nevins said in his own oral history. "I think that in the year 2000 A.D. these historians will find it a simply invaluable collection."[42] *I imagine that the most valuable sections will be those which deal with groups that are inarticulate such as the Negro, the reservation Indian and the immigrant.* Nevins wasn't interested in them. He left their stories unrecorded.

On December 2, 1947, Gould wrote to Cummings, "I managed to get a pair of glasses and lost them." Then he crossed that out, because he'd found them: "Bespectacled apologies!!!"[43] Muriel Gardiner had stopped paying his rent, and he was unraveling again. On December 8, Ezra Pound's son Omar met Gould at Cummings's house.

"O.P. sez Jo iz nuts," Pound wrote to Cummings. "Wot erbout this?"

"The question Is Joe Gould Crazy strikes me as, putting it very mildly, irrelevant," Cummings wrote back. "For 'crazy' implies either(crazy) or(not)."[44]

And then, once again, Professor Sea Gull disappeared.

12

We over estimate the past because only the permanent things remain.

—JOSEPH F. GOULD

He stopped writing. Something had finally stayed his pen.

He spent the last years of his life in Pilgrim State Hospital in Islip, the largest mental hospital in the world.[1] I don't know what was done to him there. When I asked the hospital for his medical records, citing a federal law that releases those kinds of records fifty years after the patient's death, the hospital declined my request, citing a New York State policy that effectively protects not Gould's privacy but the hospital's.[2]

Gould's confinement at Pilgrim State coincided with the most troubling era in the troubling history of the treatment of mental illness. He was in terrible shape to begin with, and he had no one to defend him against a series of remarkably disastrous medical experiments.[3]

Pilgrim State Hospital opened in 1931.[4] Its staff began administering electroshock treatments in 1940, and within four months had performed 1,610 procedures. Patients suffering from manic depression responded best, the hospital's director, Harry J. Worthing, reported, psychotics less well; the longer the patient had been afflicted with a mental disorder, the less successful the treatment, but it was nevertheless used for years on those for whom "recovery cannot be anticipated," because "electric shock therapy is cheap and easy to perform" and leaves difficult patients "quieter and more manageable."[5] In 1945, doctors at Pilgrim began conducting prefrontal lobotomies and launched a formal two-year study in 1947. Their research set the standard for the procedure. By the end of the study, 350 patients had been lobotomized. Sixty-seven had gone home; the rest were either still in the hospital or dead. But this counted as success, since what Worthing reported was relief from the previous treatment ("chronic sedation and restraint") and a mitigation of pain: after the surgery, patients suffered less, because they felt less.[6] "Cases are chosen primarily on the basis of their intractable course and the resistance to the usual procedures," Worthing explained, and those chosen included patients who were considered "shock-resistant"; that is, they "showed rapid regressive and withdrawal symptoms with massive content and emotional loss of a malignant pattern after failure of adequate shock."[7] These patients, though, tended to be the most undone by the surgery:

> Following the operation, there is normally some degree of torpid restfulness and slowness to initiate action. This is more marked and continues longer in regressed schizophrenics. Such a regressed patient may for days or even weeks, when seated before a tray of food, merely stare at it; but, if his hand is guided to start the process of eating, he will continue and even eat excessively in a rather automatic fashion.[8]

As with electroshock treatment, lobotomy was recommended even for patients for whom no recovery was expected, since it made them easier to manage.[9] By 1948, doctors at Pilgrim were lobotomizing more than two hundred patients a year.[10] The American Psychiatric Association honored Worthing for his "Successful Inauguration of Enlightened Psycho-Surgical Treatment and Rehabilitation Programs for Patients Formerly Considered Incurable."[11]

Gould would almost certainly have been given electroshock treatments, and when that failed, the next step would have been a lobotomy.[12] The consent of the patient was not required; a lobotomy, like electroshock, could be conducted by force. Worthing reported the case of a man who was exactly Gould's age, and very much meets his description:

Case No. 231. Aged 57, this man was diagnosed dementia praecox, paranoid, onset "more than 10 years ago." There were delusions of persecution, economic incapacity, withdrawal from the family, letters to authorities. He was admitted to Pilgrim State Hospital in 1947. In the hospital, he was furiously resistive, actively hallucinated, resentful, grandiose, unapproachable. Attempts to administer electric shock resulted in such combat that cardiac collapse was feared, in view of his age. Finally, he went on a hunger strike for several months and resisted tube-feeding so violently that this procedure was undertaken very reluctantly. Death seemed likely. Lobotomy was done on February 8, 1949, followed by the immediate cessation of the hunger strike. The patient admitted that he had been "imagining things." He became friendly and approachable. On close examination, residual psychotic content was noted. There was cessation of paranoid letter-writing. This man was released June 4, 1949. On first report, he was comfortable, but economically dependent. He was well-behaved. "No loss of intelligence in conversation" was observed, but "no will to work."[13]

Was Case No. 231 Joseph Ferdinand Gould? On December 2, 1947, Gould had written to Cummings: "Bespectacled apologies!!!" In May 1949, he sent a pained letter to William Carlos Williams: "I am now slowly coming to life again. I will have to rewrite a great deal of my history. That scares me as I seem to have lost much of my initial urge."[14] Between those dates, no letter in his hand survives. After that, Gould wrote three letters and one postcard—all in 1949—and then, as far as I can tell, none ever again. *There was cessation of paranoid letter-writing.*

He didn't remain out of the hospital for long. *On close examination, residual psychotic content was noted.* In February 1950, he was admitted to Bellevue. He listed Dwight Macdonald as his nearest relation.[15]

In October 1951, Colleen Chassan, the daughter of Gould's sister, Hilda, who had grown up not knowing that she had an uncle, read about him in *McSorley's Wonderful Saloon*. She went to every place Mitchell had mentioned in "Professor Sea Gull," trying to find Gould. Finally, she saw him. "He was very dirty, his suit was too large," she remembered. "His nose was running, and he didn't do anything about it." He had difficulty speaking. She said, "I felt that I had come too late."[16]

In 1952, Gould collapsed on the street. He was admitted to Columbus Hospital, and transferred to Pilgrim.[17] He never left.

Beginning in 1954, lobotomy was supplanted by psychiatry's modern regime: psychopharmacology. "Between 1945 and 1955, holes were drilled in the skulls of sixteen hundred intractably ill patients, in each of whom certain bundles of frontal brain fibres were severed," the psychologist Morton M. Hunt reported in *The New Yorker*, in "Pilgrim's Progress," a two-part series about the changes at Pilgrim:

> One out of four patients so treated was later able to leave the hospital, though the operation rendered a small percentage of the discharged men and women doltish. The rest had to remain, but a third of them behaved considerably better than they had previously. And still the population of mental hospitals in New York, which had quadrupled in fifty years, kept growing—and growing so rapidly that the state was unable to keep pace by

building new hospitals. Then, late in 1954 . . .
the state mental hospitals began testing chlor-
promazine and reserpine, the first of the tran-
quilizing drugs, and found them remarkably
effective in many cases. In 1955, the drugs
started to be used widely, and the effect was
immediate.[18]

Hunt told the story Pilgrim State Hospital
wanted him to tell: the miracle of tranquilizers
had made lobotomy obsolete. When Hunt visited
Pilgrim, though, he did meet one patient who had
been treated with both all of the old therapies
(electroshock, lobotomy) and the new drugs (each
of the tranquilizers) and yet remained insane.
"He's an interesting patient of a kind you don't
see much of any more," a nurse named Preston
told Hunt. "Would you like to meet him? He's
harmless, of course, and loves to talk about himself." Everyone called him "Professor":

He was wearing an ordinary green sports
shirt and brown slacks, a Paisley scarf about
his throat, an Indian headband with a single
dirty white sea-gull feather sticking up out of
it, and spectacles. After a moment, I noticed
that his spectacles had no lenses, and that his
mustache was white at the roots and had obvi-
ously been blackened with some homemade
dye, perhaps shoe polish. "Good afternoon,

Professor," Miss Preston said. "I'd like you to meet one of our visitors."

"It is a pleasure to meet you," he declared, in a resonant, theatrical voice. "Would you like to hear about my garden?"

I said that indeed I would.

He then pointed to two wooden crosses, embellished with ornaments of rolled-up aluminum foil, paper, and sea-gull feathers, in the center of his garden. "Now, these," he said, "I designed these myself."[19]

This professor with his sea-gull feathers wasn't Joe Gould. By the time *The New Yorker* published "Pilgrim's Progress," Gould was dead. But maybe this professor was Hunt's memory of a man he'd once known, or even visited, with Joseph Mitchell.

Most of Gould's old friends didn't know where he'd gone, but Mitchell did. One night, Ed Gottlieb, managing editor of the *Long Island Press*, called Mitchell at home. "Said he had heard that Joe Gould was dead and wanted to verify it," Mitchell wrote in his notes. "Told him Gould wasn't dead but in a mental institution." Gottlieb said he wanted to get in touch with him. Mitchell wrote in his notes, "Trying to put him off, told him that I didn't know which mental institution but would find out."[20]

At Pilgrim, Gould was very far gone. He wrote not a word.

"You solve the problem of escape by being an expatriate," he'd once written Pound. "I am an extemporate." He believed that he lived outside of time.[21] He believed he'd escaped.

On Monday, August 19, 1957, Harry J. Worthing, M.D., director of Pilgrim State Hospital, sent a telegram to Slater Brown. Joseph Ferdinand Gould was no more. "IF YOU CAN CARE FOR THE REMAINS OR KNOW THE WHEREABOUTS OF HIS FAMILY PLEASE CONTACT HOS IMMEDIATELY."[22] He left no will.[23] Mitchell got the news by telephone from Gottlieb:

> We spoke for a few minutes about how sad it was, and then I asked him if Gould had left any papers.
> "No," he said. "None at all. As the man at the hospital said, 'Not a scratch.'"[24]

On Wednesday, a writer friend of Gould's went to see Mitchell at *The New Yorker* and asked him to deliver the eulogy at Gould's funeral; Mitchell said he'd be out of town.[25] On Thursday morning, black-bordered placards were posted in shopwindows all over Greenwich Village:

Announcement to
Friends of
JOE GOULD

His funeral will be held
in the chapel at
Frank E. Campbell's
Funeral Home
81st Street and Madison Avenue
On Friday, August 23
At 11 A.M.[26]

That night, another friend of Gould's called Mitchell at home and asked him, again, to deliver the eulogy; Mitchell again said no.[27] The funeral was held the next morning.[28] *Time* ran an obituary: "Gould had no known relatives but many friends, including Poet E. E. Cummings, Artist Don Freeman, Writers Malcolm Cowley and William Saroyan."[29] None of them showed up for his funeral.[30]

The search for "The Oral History of Our Time" began straightaway. It went on for years. On August 20, the editor of the *New York World-Telegram and Sun* sent a letter to Cummings: "Gould always said that he wanted his Oral History of the World printed posthumously. . . . Could you tell me perhaps where I could locate it?"[31]

Mitchell's own, secret search began on September 10, 1957, when he ran into a man named De Hirsh Margules. They went out for coffee. Margules had known Gould. He was not unlike Gould. He told Mitchell that "he had been working on a poem for thirty-one years." Mitchell went with Margules to his apartment on Christopher

Street; Margules read him pages of the poem. One thing led to another. Mitchell saw Margules again a couple of weeks later. Margules told him to try the artist Vivian Marquie. "Mrs. Marquie gave me Rothschild's number," Mitchell wrote in his notes. "Rothschild gave me the Neel, Feist, and Buttinger numbers." Through them, he found Muriel Gardiner.[32]

Gould's niece, Colleen Chassan, hired a family friend named Mary L. Holman to help her find her uncle's lost work.[33] Holman sent queries to the Harvard Library and to the Smithsonian.[34] Then, quietly, Mitchell took over Holman's search. He searched for years. He must have been so haunted.

The public hunt for "The Oral History of Our Time" was led by Lawrence Woodman and James Nalbud, two fairly sketchy characters, who tried to recruit Mitchell and failed.[35] (Woodman claimed to be related to Gould but was not; Nalbud's name is his actual name, Dublan, spelled backward.) Nalbud tried to get the Ford Foundation to sponsor the search. "If I find the papers," he told Mitchell, "maybe the foundation will give me a grant to put them in order for publication."[36] In April 1958, Nalbud sent a letter to *The Harvard Crimson*, inviting Harvard undergraduates to join a treasure hunt: "The search is for the resources of a legacy to your University which have been lost, strayed, or stolen. The value of this legacy is priceless."[37] The Harvard Library conducted an investigation and determined that no such gift had ever been arranged.[38] Nalbud began posting flyers all over New York, offering a twenty-five-dollar reward for any leads.[39] He sent letters asking recipients to fill out and return a form typed on a postcard:

RE: JOE GOULD'S LOST MMS.

What was the largest number of Joe's
    note books you saw? _____
In crates, suitcases, bales, loose (check)
Did you examine and read any of the
    books? _____
Did you at any time own or store any of
    the books? _____
Date _____ Name _____[40]

The last clue comes from Ezra Pound, in a letter he sent from St. Elizabeth's. On April 14, 1958, Pound wrote to Cummings, "am doin wot I kan to hellup yr friends edit Joe Gould."[41] Edit what? Did Pound have the notebooks? Four days later, Pound was released.

Near the end, I found in the archives a chapter of Joe Gould's Oral History called "Why I Write." It held an answer to the question I'd started with. "If one were to pick anyone up at random and study him intensely enough in all the ramifications of his life, we would get the whole story of man," he wrote.[42]

What is biography? A life in time.

Augusta Savage hid, and tried to erase every last trace of herself, but she never really got free of Joe Gould's hold. In 1960, a man walked into the Schomburg Center for Research in Black Culture, on 135th Street, and tried to walk out with the bust of W. E. B. Du Bois that Savage had made thirty-seven years before. Stopped at the door, he surrendered it. He said Savage had sent him. Later that year, the bust disappeared. It has never been found.[43]

Augusta Savage died in poverty and obscurity in 1962.[44] Her work had been, at best, uneven. Counting only her best-known sculptures, she produced more than seventy major pieces. Later, when the Schomburg Center prepared to stage an exhibit, its curators could find only nineteen.[45] Some people believe she collected as much of her work as she could, and smashed it.

When *The New Yorker* published "Joe Gould's Secret" in 1964, it made many readers weep.[46] It made many others terribly, terribly curious. "It has occurred to me that when Gould collapsed on the street in 1952 and was taken to Columbus Hospital, he may have had the Oral History with him, and it may, to this day, be in the lockers there where patients' belongings are kept," a

nurse wrote to Mitchell, breathlessly, after reading the story. "I wonder if Columbus Hospital
has been checked about the History. Also, he may
have taken it with him to Bellevue—and it may
still be there, molding away in some cupboard.
Or it may be at Pilgrim State. If these hospitals
haven't been checked, I think it well worthwhile
to make such an effort, don't you?"[47]

Shouldn't someone check?

Not me.

Instead, I went to Saugerties. Augusta Savage's
farm is still there, and the ruins of her studio, and
her scant remains: her chamber pot, her typewriter, and a book of poems inscribed to her by the
author, "For my fellow artist Augusta Savage—in
admiration and regard, James Weldon Johnson."
Lift every voice. Her Flit gun is still there, too,
gathering dust, turning to rust, in a house not
far from what's now called Augusta Savage Road.
Outside her kitchen, dug into the ground, there's
a cistern, deep enough to drown a man.

Epilogue

Summer came, and stillness. I packed my stacks of notes and photocopies into a box. His school transcripts. The Gould Family Pedigree. His Guggenheim application. The diaries, the letters, the letters, the letters. Photographs of Augusta Savage's work: *The New Negro, Mourning Victory.* A copy of Harry J. Worthing et al., "350 Cases of Prefrontal Lobotomy," in *Psychiatric Quarterly.* I dragged the box into a closet. I carried my books back to the library: discharged.

I spoke on the telephone to an old man in a faraway land. He told me he had some of Gould's notebooks. I believed him. I did not call him again.

I still sometimes picture a door with the word "Archive" etched on smoky glass. I picture it like this. Allen Ginsberg is lurking in the hallway, muttering to himself in a haze of smoke, "I saw the best minds of my generation destroyed by madness, starving hysterical naked, / dragging themselves through the negro streets at dawn." I sneak past him; he doesn't notice. I open the door and shut it soundlessly behind me. I expect the room to be enormous, and empty, and silent, and it is very big, but cluttered and blaring. The walls had once been painted white and the floor had been covered with a linoleum as green as the sea, but I can see only trickles of white and hardly any green. Handwriting, in black ink, curls across the floor and crawls up the walls.

I kneel down to read what's written on the threshold: *The Race Question.* It's the title of a pedigree chart that, starting there, at the door, has been drawn on the floor. It begins in 1619 with the rape of an unnamed African woman by an Englishman named John Blye. Across the floor, circles hitched to squares beget circles and squares, darker, lighter, lighter, darker.

On one side of the room, an 1889 Edison phonograph rests on a sideboard, its cylinder turning, its brass trumpet blasting a single sound, over and over again: *Scree-eek!* Near the sideboard, hundreds of black-and-white composition books have been stacked to form an unsteady, tottering tower, seven feet high. I back away from the tower and almost fall over a cardboard box tied with string and marked "Norwood Dump."

In a corner, there's an iron cage. Inside the cage is an old radio in a cabinet made of walnut, like a mantel clock. The radio is broadcasting Ezra Pound from Radio Rome. "Scree-eek!" says the phonograph. *"You let in the Jew . . . ,"* says the radio. "Scree-eek!" says the phonograph.

In the middle of the room, beneath a vaulted glass ceiling, a gigantic white sheet covers something hulking. I lift off the sheet to unveil a sculpture made of plaster, sixteen feet high, and lacquered black: a harp, with each of its twelve strings capped by the head of a child, mouth open in song. The label reads:

> Augusta Savage, *Lift Every Voice and Sing (The Harp)*, 1939. Made for the World's Fair. Destroyed in 1940, due to lack of storage space.

I leave the sheet on the floor.

In the back of the room, a rickety bed leans along a wall, a cot, the size of an examination table, bare except for an old overcoat, tattered and stained and pocked with cigarette burns. I inventory the nightstand: a Flit gun; a bottle of whiskey; a pair of spectacles, shattered; and a book by Muriel Gardiner, *The Wolf-Man and Professor Sea Gull.*

Shoved into the farthest, darkest corner of the room there's a heavy oak desk and an empty oak chair. On top of the desk sits Joseph Mitchell's typewriter and, curled in its roller, a piece of *New Yorker* stationery, blank. A Milton Bradley color top rests on a pile of newspapers and magazines: an old *Harvard Crimson*, a *New Republic.* Beside it is a bottle of ink, a fountain pen, and one last dime-store notebook, its black cover mottled like the pelt of a speckled goat. On its cover is written, *Property of* GOULD, JOE, and below that, MEO TEMPORE, THIRD VERSION. I open the notebook and read, in his unmistakable hand:

> *I would like to widen*
> *the sphere of history*
> *as Walt Whitman did*
> *that of poetry.*

I close the book.

I reach into my pocket for what I've brought. It feels like porcelain. It opens like a clam. And then I back out of that room, as soundlessly as I came, having left behind: Joe Gould's teeth.

Acknowledgments

This book, which I drafted over the course of a semester, could not have been written without the help of very many people. My students asked excellent questions. Generous archivists and librarians answered my many requests. I'm especially grateful to Nora Mitchell Sanborn, Joseph Mitchell's daughter, and to the New York Public Library, for permission to see Mitchell's papers. Karlyn Knaust Elia and Richard Duncan, owners of the Augusta Savage House and Studio in Saugerties, New York, very generously gave me a tour, and Savage's neighbors kindly shared their memories. Thanks, too, to André Bernard at the Guggenheim Foundation, who uncovered Gould's application materials, and to the Foundation for the fellowship that made it possible for me to revise the manuscript. Three of my current and former students helped out with transcription: Carla Cevasco transcribed Gould's diaries, Emmet Stackelberg transcribed Gould's correspondence with Charles Davenport, and Benjamin Naddaff-Hafrey transcribed Savage's correspondence at Fisk. Harvard colleagues guided me through disciplinary thickets. Anne Harrington helped me understand the history of psychiatry. Christina Davis at the Woodberry Poetry Room talked me through the history of sound. Robert Waldinger and Alfred Margulies, psychiatrists at the Medical School, read an early draft and provided invaluable advice about what might have afflicted Gould. Abundant thanks to all. Heartfelt thanks, too, to Adrianna Alty, to whom this book is dedicated, and to Tina Bennett, Dan Frank, Jane Kamensky, Leah Price, David Remnick, and Henry Finder.

Sources

Gould's papers are scattered in archives all over the country. As with any literary remains, they represent only a portion of the writing Gould produced. Because many people to whom Gould sent letters considered him an annoyance, or worse, most of the letters he wrote, and especially those he sent to strangers, were discarded. Even his friends and family, of course, threw his letters away. E. E. Cummings was one of his oldest friends. Most of Cummings's exchanges with Gould were face-to-face—unrecorded oral history—but, since Gould was such a compulsive letter writer, he also wrote to Cummings. Cummings kept many of the letters Gould sent him, but not all of them. For instance, on August 1, 1938, Cummings described a typical letter from Gould in a letter to his sister, Elizabeth Cummings Qualey:

> Our "little gentleman" recently honoured me
> with a letter worth anyone's weight in led (not
> to mention Geld) beginning "Dear friend"
> and plunging into Ethiopia.

This from Gould to Cummings does not survive. Nor do letters from Cummings to Gould survive, because those would have been in Gould's possession, and everything Gould ever owned he lost. Far scarcer, though, are the literary remains of Augusta Savage. It appears that Savage destroyed the great bulk of her papers. Some of her artwork remains in private hands, while other works can be found among the holdings of the Cleveland Museum of Art, Fisk University, the Schomburg Center, the Seattle Art Museum, and the Smithsonian American Art Museum.

ABBREVIATIONS

Bifur Archive	*Bifur* Archive, 1921–1930, Department of Special Collections and University Archives, McFarlin Library, University of Tulsa
Boas Papers	Franz Boas Papers, Mss.B.B61, American Philosophical Society
Braithwaite Collection	William Stanley Braithwaite Collection, 1899–1928, MSS 8990, Special Collections, University of Virginia Library
Braithwaite Papers	William Stanley Braithwaite Papers, MS Am 1444, Houghton Library, Harvard University
Brand Papers	Millen Brand Papers, 1919–1976, Rare Book and Manuscript Library, Columbia University Library

Brown Papers	Edmund R. Brown, 1934–1935, MSS 15076, Special Collections, University of Virginia Library
Cosmopolitan Club	Harvard Cosmopolitan Club, Miscellaneous, HUD 3299, Harvard University Archives
Cowley Papers	Malcolm Cowley Papers, MMS Cowley, Newberry Library, Chicago
Cullen Papers	Countee Cullen Papers, Amistad Research Center, Tulane University
Cummings Letters	Letters of E. E. Cummings and Marion Cummings, MSS 6246, Special Collections, University of Virginia Library
Cummings Papers	E. E. Cummings Papers, 1870–1969, MS Am 1823, Houghton Library, Harvard University
Cummings Papers, Additional I	E. E. Cummings Additional Papers, 1870–1969, MS Am 1892, Houghton Library, Harvard University
Cummings Papers, Additional II	E. E. Cummings Additional Papers, 1917–1962, MS Am 1892, Houghton Library, Harvard University
Cummings and Qualey Papers	E. E. Cummings letters to Elizabeth Cummings Qualey, 1917–1963, MS Am 1765, Houghton Library, Harvard University
Davenport Papers	Charles Benedict Davenport Papers, MSS B: D27, American Philosophical Society
Dial Papers	*Dial*/Scofield Thayer Papers, Beinecke Rare Book and Manuscript Library, Yale University, MSS 34

Du Bois Papers	W. E. B. Du Bois Papers, 1803–1999, MS 312, Special Collections and University Archives, University of Massachusetts, Amherst
Eugenics Record Office Papers	Eugenics Record Office, Ms. Coll. No. 77, Joseph F. Gould File, American Philosophical Society
Gardiner Reminiscences	Reminiscences of Muriel Gardiner, 1977–1982, Columbia Oral History Archives, Rare Book and Manuscript Library, Columbia University
Gould Diaries	Fales Manuscript Collection, MSS 001, Box 71, Folders 1–11, Fales Library and Special Collections, Elmer Holmes Bobst Library, New York University
Gould Guggenheim Files	Joseph F. Gould, Guggenheim Fellowship Application Files, John Simon Guggenheim Foundation Archives, New York
Gould Harvard Files	Joseph F. Gould, Undergraduate Record File, Harvard University Archives
Gould, "My Life"	Joe Gould, "My Life," a chapter of his Oral History, dated December 31, 1933, and later typewritten and redacted by Millen Brand, Brand Papers, uncataloged Box 1, Joe Gould folder
Gould, "Myself"	Joe Gould, "Myself," a chapter of his Oral History, typewritten and redacted by Millen Brand, Brand Papers, uncataloged Box 1, Joe Gould folder
Gould, "Synopsis"	Joe Gould, "Synopsis of the Oral History," 1932, Joseph Freeman Collection, Box 25, folder 10, Hoover Institution Archives

Gould, "Why I Write"	Joe Gould, "Why I Write," a chapter of his Oral History, dated 1934, and later typewritten and redacted by Millen Brand, Brand Papers, uncataloged Box 1, Joe Gould folder
Gregg Papers	Alan Gregg Papers, National Library of Medicine
Hound & Horn Records	*Hound & Horn* Records, MSS 458, Beinecke Rare Book and Manuscript Library, Yale University
Lachaise Collection	Gaston Lachaise Collection, YCAL MSS 434, Beinecke Rare Book and Manuscript Library, Yale University
Macdonald Papers	Dwight Macdonald Papers, MS 730, Manuscripts and Archives, Yale University Library
Mitchell Papers	Joseph Mitchell Papers, Manuscripts and Archives Division, New York Public Library
Mumford Papers	Lewis Mumford Papers, Ms. Coll. 2, Kislak Center for Special Collections, Rare Books and Manuscripts, University of Pennsylvania Libraries
New Directions	New Directions Publishing Corp. Records, ca. 1933–1997, MS Am 2077, Houghton Library, Harvard University
Pound Papers	Ezra Pound Papers, MSS 43, Beinecke Rare Book and Manuscript Library, Yale University
Pound/Cummings	Barry Ahearn, ed., *Pound/Cummings: The Correspondence of Ezra Pound and E. E. Cummings* (Ann Arbor: University of Michigan Press, 1996)

Pound/Williams   Hugh Witemeyer, ed., *Pound/Williams:*
                       Selected Letters of Ezra Pound and William
                       Carlos Williams (New York: New
                       Directions, 1996)

Pound/Zukofsky   Barry Ahearn, ed., *Pound/Zukofsky:*
                       Selected Letters of Ezra Pound and Louis
                       Zukofsky (New York: Faber & Faber,
                       1987)

Rosenwald   Julius Rosenwald Fund Archives,
Archives   1917–1948, Special Collections, Fisk
                       University

Savage FBI File   Surveillance Files on African American
                       Intellectuals and Activists Obtained
                       from the FBI Archives via a Freedom
                       of Information Act Request, Augusta
                       Savage Folder, Manuscripts, Archives
                       and Rare Books Division, Schomburg
                       Center for Research in Black Culture,
                       New York Public Library

Savage Papers   Augusta Savage Papers, MG 731,
                       Manuscripts, Archives and Rare Books
                       Division, Schomburg Center for
                       Research in Black Culture, New York
                       Public Library

West Papers   Dorothy West Papers, ca. 1890–1998,
                       Schlesinger Library, Radcliffe Institute,
                       Harvard University

Williams Papers   William Carlos Williams Papers, YCAL
                       MSS 116, Beinecke Rare Book and
                       Manuscript Library, Yale University

Wilson Papers   Edmund Wilson Papers, 1931–1943,
                       YCAL MSS 187, Beinecke Rare Book
                       and Manuscript Library, Yale University

Notes

1. Gould wrote about this fear all his life but see, for example, Gould to Ezra Pound, May 6, 1933, Pound Papers, Box 19, Folder 861.
2. Regarding buying supplies at five-and-dimes, see diary entry for July–August 1945, Gould Diaries.
3. Gould to George Soule, April 12, 1934, Cowley Papers, Box 106, Folder 5000. Soule was *The New Republic*'s staff economist.
4. Gould to Edmund R. Brown, May 5, 1935, Brown Papers, Barrett Minor Box 10.
5. Gould to Marianne Moore, December 12, 1928, *Dial* Papers, Box 2, Folder 80.
6. Moore to Gould, December 17, 1928, *Dial* Papers, Box 2, Folder 80.
7. Gould to George Sarton, March 1931, George Sarton Additional Papers, MS Am 1803 (655), Houghton Library, Harvard University.
8. Horace Gregory, "Pepys on the Bowery," *New Republic*, April 15, 1931.
9. Gould to Pound, January 1928, Pound Papers, Box 19, Folder 861.
10. On this movement, see Benjamin Filene, *Romancing the Folk: Public Memory and American Roots Music* (Chapel Hill: University of North Carolina Press, 2000).

11. "Writer Honors 7,300,000th Word by Party," *New York Herald Tribune*, March 2, 1936.

12. Charles Norman, "Joe Gould Writes History as He Hears It," *PM Weekly*, August 24, 1941.

13. Gould to Pound, May 30, 1938, Pound Papers, Box 19, Folder 861.

14. Cummings to Pound, May 1935, *Pound/Cummings*, 69.

15. Dwight Macdonald, Statement on Joe Gould, unpublished eleven-page typewritten essay, Macdonald Papers, Box 78, Folder 142.

16. Norman, "Joe Gould Writes History as He Hears It."

17. William Saroyan, "How I Met Joe Gould," *Don Freeman's Newsstand* 1 (1941): 25, 27.

18. Joseph Mitchell, "Professor Sea Gull," *New Yorker*, December 12, 1942.

19. Barbara C. Kroll to Joseph Mitchell, March 10, 1968, Mitchell Papers, Box 9.1. Kroll was recalling reading "Professor Sea Gull," as a college student, in 1942.

20. Ved Mehta to Joseph Mitchell, undated, 1964, Mitchell Papers, Box 9.1. This is after "Joe Gould's Secret" appeared.

21. Calvin Trillin, foreword to *McSorley's Wonderful Saloon*, by Joseph Mitchell (New York: Pantheon, 2001).

22. The comparison to Joyce was commonly made. See, e.g., "I felt I was truly immersed in the American Ulysses": Sherman Chickering to Joseph Mitchell, October 23, 1964, Mitchell Papers, Box 9.1 (Chickering was describing reading "Joe Gould's Secret").

23. Mitchell, "Professor Sea Gull."

24. Gould, "A Chapter from Joe Gould's Oral History: Art," *Exile*, November 1927, 116.

25. Edward J. O'Brien, letter of recommendation for Joe Gould, 1934, Gould Guggenheim Files; Pound,

Editor's Note, *Exile*, November 1927, 118–19; Gould to Pound, January 1928, Pound Papers, Box 19, Folder 861.

26. Gould to Williams, August 7, 1947, Cummings Papers, Folder 490; Diary entry for July 26, 1943, Gould Diaries; Gould to Cummings, December 2, 1947, Cummings Papers, Folder 490; Cummings to Pound, March 1, 1930, *Pound/Cummings*, 18.

27. Gould to Williams, December 16, 1932, Williams Papers, Box 7, Folder 243; Gould to Lewis Mumford, January 1941, Mumford Papers, Box 23, Folder 1906; Cummings to Elizabeth Cummings Qualey, March 9, 1950, Cummings and Qualey Papers, Box 1, Folder 23; Gould to Mumford, December 22, 1941, Mumford Papers, Box 23, Folder 1906.

28. Diary entry for May 8, 1943, Gould Diaries. Gould fell in January 1943 and was unable to write about it until after his recovery. And see Slater Brown to Joseph Mitchell, April 8, 1943, Mitchell Papers, Box 9.1.

29. Diary entry for March 23, 1944, Gould Diaries.

30. Linda [no last name], undated but 1964, Mitchell Papers, Box 9.1.

31. Mitchell, "Joe Gould's Secret," *New Yorker*, September 19 and 26, 1964.

CHAPTER 2

1. Diary entries for August 6, 1945; April 11, 1945; December 5, 1944; December 17, 1944; January 30, 1945; and February 3, 1945, Gould Diaries. On stealing ink from the post office, see Mitchell's 1942 research notes, Mitchell Papers, Box 9.1.

2. Gould, "Meo Tempore: A Selection from Joe Gould's Oral History," *Pagany* 2 (1931): 96–99; quotation from 97.

3. Joseph Mitchell, *Joe Gould's Secret* (New York: Vintage, 1965; New York: Modern Library, 2000).
4. Mitchell, "Professor Sea Gull."
5. Mitchell, "Joe Gould's Secret."
6. Gould to William Braithwaite, October 14, 1911, Braithwaite Collection, Box 8, Folder of Joseph F. Gould.
7. Alice W. Barker to Mitchell, August 16, 1943, Mitchell Papers, Box 9.1.
8. "She hated him then," Hilda Gould's daughter told Mitchell, decades later, "and she still hates him." Colleen Chassan interview, August 3, 1959, Mitchell Papers, Box 9.1.
9. Mitchell, "Professor Sea Gull." An essay titled "Why I Am Called Professor Sea Gull" is one of the very last things Gould ever wrote. See Gould to Williams, May 1949, Williams Papers, Box 7, Folder 243. After Gould's death in 1957, Chris Cominel, a staff writer for the *New York World-Telegram and Sun*, spent a day looking for Gould's Oral History; all he was able to find was this essay. Chris Cominel, "Gould Saved from Potter's Field but His History Is Lost," *New York World-Telegram and Sun*, August 22, 1957.
10. I have tried to avoid diagnosing Gould, because, on evidentiary grounds, it's impossible and because, as a matter of historical method, it's unsupportable. But I did consult with two psychiatrists at Harvard Medical School, Robert J. Waldinger and Alfred S. Margulies, and both offered invaluable advice. Robert Waldinger, email to the author, May 17, 2015; Alfred Margulies, email to the author, June 1, 2015.
11. Gould, "My Life," 1.
12. He mentions this in his application to work at the Eugenics Record Office: Eugenics Record Office Papers, Joseph F. Gould File. There was a public telephone (one of six in the town of Norwood) at

483 Washington Street, across the street from the Goulds' house at 486 Washington Street. New England Telephone & Telegraph Co., advertisement, *Resident and Business Directory of Norwood and Walpole, Massachusetts, 1906* (Boston: Boston Suburban Book Co., 1906), 32; Gould's father also had a private telephone in his office, on the first floor of his house, at a time when very few people in Norwood had a private line (see the listing in that same directory): "GOULD, CLARKE S., physician and surgeon, 486 Washington, h.do. Office hours from 1 to 3 and 6 to 9 p.m. Tel. 51-3." Gould also later explained that the Oral History would draw from "diaries of the period when I was in charge of the telephone service at Squantum." Gould, "Synopsis," 6. He is referring here to the Harvard Aviation Field, founded at Squantum Point in Quincy, Massachusetts, in 1910; in 1917 it became the Naval Air Station Squantum. Gould said the Oral History would include "accounts of the two Harvard Aviation Meets in 1910 and 1912."

13. Gould, entrance exam record, Gould Harvard Files.

14. Gould, "Myself," 2.

15. Gould, "My Life," 2.

16. [Dean Byron S. Hurlbut] to Clarke S. Gould, February 21, 1908; [Hurlbut] to Joseph F. Gould, February 29, May 26, and November 8, 1908; Mr. L. Allard [to Hurlbut], February 8, 1908; [Hurlbut] to Clarke S. Gould, March 4, 1908; and Robert Matteson Johnston to [unspecified dean], January 11, 1913 ("I saw Joseph F. Gould this morning, who wanted to complete History 27, which he failed to complete in 1910–11, simply by a thesis"), Gould Harvard Files. History 27 was "The Historical Literature of France and England Since the Close of the Eighteenth Century." *Harvard University Catalogue, 1910–1911* (Cambridge, MA: Harvard University, 1910), 334.

17. Hurlbut to Gould, November 3, 1909; Hurlbut to

Gould, October 17, 1910; E. H. Wells to Clarke Storer Gould, July 10, 1911, Gould Harvard Files.

18. Clarke Storer Gould to E. H. Wells, August 1, 1911, Gould Harvard Files.

CHAPTER 3

1. Gould, "Synopsis."

2. Mitchell's interview notes with Gould, 1942, Mitchell Papers, Box 9.1.

3. Charles Norman, "Joe Gould Writes History as He Hears It," *PM Weekly*, August 24, 1941.

4. O'Brien, letter of recommendation for Joe Gould, 1934, Gould Guggenheim Files.

5. Gould, "My Life," 2.

6. Brown and Gould had known one another as children, and during Gould's junior year of college he lived with Brown's family in Cambridge, on Rutland Street. Gould, "My Life," 1–2. Gould reports that in 1905 he worked with Brown as assistant editor of a little magazine called *Freak*.

7. W. E. B. Du Bois, *The Souls of Black Folk* (1903). And see Kwame Anthony Appiah, *Lines of Descent: W. E. B. Du Bois and the Emergence of Identity* (Cambridge, MA: Harvard University Press, 2014).

8. Gould, "How Does Race Prejudice Affect Race Purity?," *Boston Globe*, June 25, 1911. The essay was part of a forum on the subject. Another contributor was the white supremacist William Benjamin Smith, professor of philosophy at Tulane, who argued that miscegenation was a grave threat to humanity. William Benjamin Smith, "Lower and Higher Races," *Boston Globe*, June 25, 1911. And see Smith, *The Color Line: A Brief in Behalf of the Unborn* (New York: McClure, Phillips & Co., 1905).

9. "Such a feeling seems confined to rather nervous

people, or those with intellectual specialization." Gould to Davenport, November 14, 1913, Davenport Papers. "I have had quite a correspondence with Doctor Charles Eastman," Gould later wrote. I have not been able to find that correspondence. Gould to Davenport, August 29, 1915, Davenport Papers.

10. Gould to Braithwaite, October 14, 1911, Braithwaite Collection, Box 8, Folder of Joseph F. Gould; Gould, "Synopsis," 4–5; Diary entry for October 5, 1945, Gould Diaries.

11. Gould to Hurlbut, January 22, 1912, Gould Harvard Files. Under pressure from Gould's father, the university had relented and allowed for the presentation of such a petition. E. H. Wells to Clarke Storer Gould, September 26, 1911. Gould's behavior was bizarre. He asked at least one professor for money. Gould to Hurlbut, January 26, 1912, Gould Harvard Files. "J.F. Gould is engaged in literary work," he reported to Harvard in 1912 when he got back to Massachusetts. *Secretary's First Report, Harvard College Class of 1911* (Cambridge, MA: Crimson Printing Co., 1912).

12. Joseph F. Gould, "Report of Census Enumerator," *42nd Annual Report, Town of Norwood, Year Ending December 31, 1913* (Norwood, MA, 1914), 327, and "Report of Census Enumerator," *43rd Annual Report, Town of Norwood, Year Ending December 31, 1914* (Norwood, MA, 1915), 219. Joseph F. Gould, "Racial Survey of Norwood, Parts I–IX," *Norwood Messenger*, July 5, 12, 19, and 26, 1913; August 2, 9, and 16, 1913; September 20, 1913; and October 4, 1913. (My thanks to Patricia Fanning of the Norwood Historical Society for sharing these with me.) On the lecture, see the printed postcard announcing Mr. Joseph F. Gould's lecture at the Boston Scientific Society, November 26, 1912, Joseph F. Gould, Quadrennial File, Harvard University Archives. The

biography of Gould offered here is: "Mr. Gould, a Contributing Editor of the Four Seas is a Harvard man who has taken much interest in conditions of men. He has studied them in their own environment having made a walking tour of five hundred miles in Canada studying Lumberjacks, Indians and other types. He is president of the Race Pride League."

13. [Hurlbut or Wells] to Gould, January 23, 1913; Gould to Hurlbut, May 15, 1913; Gould to Hurlbut, November 30, 1913. He may have expected to extract a certain vengeance in the Oral History, which, he later said, would include much material on the Harvard faculty: "I have a good chapter on President Lowell of Harvard. In time I expect to add chapters on other members of the Harvard faculty." Gould, "Synopsis," 7.

14. *Poetry Journal* 1 (1912): 1, and *Poetry Journal* 3 (1914): 183.

15. Gould to Nino Frank, December 29, 1929, *Bifur* Archive, Box 1, Folder 13; and Pound. Gould to Pound from Hotel Bradford, January [or June?], 1928, Pound Papers, Box 19, Folder 861. O'Brien died in 1941. "When he died, his executor and secretary destroyed almost everything." Ingeborg O'Brien, email to the author, April 26, 2015.

16. Jack Levitz to Mitchell, November 13, 1964, Mitchell Papers, Box 9.1.

17. Mitchell, note, November 1964, Mitchell Papers, Box 9.1.

18. Israel G. Young to Dr. Theodore Grieder, NYU Special Collections, November 18, 1967, and Theodore Grieder, "Joe Gould's Notebooks," unpublished five-page typescript, Fales Manuscript Collection, MSS 001, Box 71, Folder 1.

19. Diary entry for January 1, 1943, Gould Diaries.

20. Diary entry for May 21, 1943, Gould Diaries.

21. Diary entry for June 5, 1945, Gould Diaries.

22. Gould had written to Gregg to ask him to become a member of the Oral History Society, adding, "It is also possible that you might be able to help me find a better place for storing my manuscripts than I have at present. Twice they have been jeopardized by fire." When Gregg was in New York, he made an appointment with Gould. Gould never showed up. Gould to Alan Gregg, 1940, Gregg Papers, and see Gould's later diary entries about Gregg. Gregg was the director of the Rockefeller Foundation's medical sciences program. That a psychiatrist held this position suggests how much of American psychiatry became experimental in the 1930s and 1940s. Gregg, much influenced by Adolf Meyer, was essentially a psychobiologist. See Jack Pressman, *Last Resort: Psychosurgery and the Limits of Medicine* (New York: Cambridge University Press, 1998), 30–46.

23. Gould's fixation on the question of whether it was normal or abnormal to be sexually attracted to people of other races had led him to write endless letters to the country's best-known authorities on racial mixing, including Henry Goddard, a psychologist who advocated intelligence testing, and Charles Eastman, a Dakota Indian with European forebears. "Dr. Goddard writes me that race-prejudice is unknown among idiots. Primitive people seem not to have it. The Indian frequently shares the social prejudice against the Negro, but Dr. Charles A. Eastman tells me that as far as he knows the Indian has no real antipathy or 'phobia' for other racial groups." Gould to Davenport, November 14, 1913, Davenport Papers. "I have had quite a correspondence with Doctor Charles Eastman," Gould later wrote. I have not been able to find that correspondence. Gould to Davenport, August 29, 1915, Davenport Papers.

24. Gould to Franz Boas, misdated by an archivist as

December 31, 1920, but plainly September 1920, Boas Papers. "No one has ever been able to make head or tail of the Albanian episode," Malcolm Cowley said. Mitchell's 1942 interview notes, Mitchell Papers, Box 9.1.

25. Boas to Gould, September 21, 1920. Gould wrote again (undated but September 1920), at still greater length. Boas replied, on October 2, 1920, with a single sentence: "If you want to talk to me about this subject that interests you, I shall be glad to see you. Kindly telephone me so that we can make an appointment." Boas Papers.

26. "Variation and Heredity" is described in the *Harvard University Catalogue, 1910–1911*. Gould got a C. Gould Harvard Files. Gould to Davenport, June 6, 1914, Davenport Papers.

27. Charles Davenport, *Eugenics: The Science of Human Improvement by Better Breeding* (New York: H. Holt & Co., 1910); and see Davenport, *Heredity in Relation to Eugenics* (New York: H. Holt & Co., 1911).

28. Gould to Davenport, November 14, 1913, Davenport Papers.

29. Davenport to Gould, December 29, 1913; and Gould to Davenport, January 3, 1914, Davenport Papers.

CHAPTER 4

1. Davenport to Gould, January 5, 1914, Davenport Papers.

2. Gould to Davenport, January 11, 1915, Davenport Papers.

3. Gould to Davenport, October 16, 1913, Davenport Papers.

4. Ibid.

5. Davenport's proposed visit happened to fall on the day of a suffrage parade that Gould had pledged to

attend. "It will be a valid excuse for reneging," Gould
wrote Davenport, delighted. "It seems to me that
because biological specialization seems to increase
sex-differences with increased civilisation that woman
will need to enlarge her interests to keep the psychi-
cal gulf between the sexes from widening. So you
see I might get into trouble in the parade." Gould
to Davenport, April 15, 1914, Davenport Papers.

6. The courses Gould tried to get into in 1914 were
many. See Hurlbut's letters to several instructors,
May 1, 1914, and the replies to Gould, May 6, 1914.
Professor Gustavus Howard Maynadier allowed him
to take the examination in English 37, "The Story
of King Arthur," without attending a single lecture.
Hurlbut to G. H. Maynadier, April 9, 1914, Gould
Harvard Files. For the course, see the *Harvard University Catalogue, 1913–1914* (Cambridge, MA: Harvard University, 1913), 331. Gould passed the exam.
Gould to Hurlbut, January 2, 1915, and Hurlbut
to Gould, January 4, 1915, Gould Harvard Files.

7. Gould to Davenport, April 25, 1914, Davenport
Papers. The Cosmopolitan Club was founded in
1908. John Reed was the founding president. After
Reed graduated, the next president was D. C. Gupta,
from Bengal. "Cosmopolitan Club Officers," *Harvard Bulletin*, June 1909. See Henry Wilder Foote,
letter to the editor, *Harvard Bulletin*, November
1907; Cosmopolitan Club, *Harvard Bulletin*, June
1908; Membership certificate, 1909, Cosmopolitan
Club Papers; and "Cosmopolitan Club," *Harvard
Bulletin*, June 1910; "Harvard Cosmopolitan Club,"
Harvard Bulletin, May 1911. Gould told people he
had been a member. See, for example, Edward Nagel
and Slater Brown, "Joseph Gould: The Man," *Broom*
5 (October 1923): 145–46. But I have not been able to
find Gould's name on any list of members. Harvard
Cosmopolitan Club, May 12, 1909, Harvard Cos-

mopolitan Club, Miscellaneous, HUD 3299, Harvard University Archives.

8. Gould to Davenport, November 14, 1913, and November 1, 1914, Davenport Papers.

9. "I am not going to assume any editorial task, but I am going to suggest to Prof. William E. Castle that he try and help the eugenics movement to some of the publicity of which it stands in need." Gould to Davenport, January 11, 1915, Davenport Papers.

10. For example, Joseph F. Gould, "In Moslem Spain," *Crisis* 7 (April 1914): 289–300.

11. Upton Sinclair, ed., *The Cry for Justice: An Anthology of the Literature of Social Protest* (Philadelphia: John C. Winston Co., 1915); Sinclair acknowledges Gould for helping with the manuscript, 20.

12. "ONE PRISONER, A STUDENT OF RACIAL CONDITIONS," *Boston Herald*, April 19, 1915.

13. Joseph F. Gould, "Equality of Opportunity Is the Chief Safeguard of Racial Opportunity," *Proceedings of the Sagamore Sociological Conference, Sagamore, Massachusetts, June 30–July 2, 1914* (Sagamore, MA, 1917), 57–58. Gould was on the Platform Committee, 33. "What is the race question?" Gould asked at Sagamore in 1914. "It seems to me a conflict between two ideals—the American ideal of democracy, and the instinctive desire of any specialized people to keep their racial integrity intact." History, he said, shows that "there is least intermixture where two races meet on equal terms," and therefore, "those who desire racial purity should put forth their efforts to abolish discrimination."

14. Gould, "My Life," 2. Perlstein spoke at the same Sagamore conference.

15. Gould to Davenport, January 11, 1915, Davenport Papers; Gould to Hurlbut, January 28, 1915, Gould Harvard Files; Gould to Davenport, September 24, 1915, Davenport Papers.

16. "ONE PRISONER, A STUDENT OF RACIAL CONDITIONS," *Boston Herald*, April 19, 1915; Gould, "My Life," 3.

17. Joseph F. Gould, application, examination, pedigree, and supporting materials, Eugenics Record Office Papers.

18. Davenport to Gould, September 14, 1915, Davenport Papers.

19. Milton Bradley, *Elementary Color* (Springfield, MA: Milton Bradley Co., 1895), 31–34. For a discussion of Davenport's use of the top, see Michael Keevak, *Becoming Yellow: A Short History of Racial Thinking* (Princeton, NJ: Princeton University Press, 2011), 89–100.

20. Gould to Davenport, October 19, 1915, Davenport Papers. And see Gould to Abbott Lawrence Lowell, November 22, 1915, Records of the President of Harvard University, Abbott Lawrence Lowell, 1909–1933, Box 79, Folder 857, Harvard University Archives, UAI 5.160. Gould also chronicled his time in the Dakotas in a set of detailed letters to the editor of his hometown newspaper. See Joseph F. Gould, "A Norwoodite in No. Dakota," *Norwood Messenger*, March 23, 1916 (printing a letter to the editor dated February 25, 1916); "A Norwoodite in No. Dakota," *Norwood Messenger*, April 1, 1916 (printing a letter to the editor dated February 27, 1916); and "A Norwoodite in No. Dakota," *Norwood Messenger*, May 13, 1916 (printing a letter to the editor dated April 14, 1916). The letters are especially interesting because they're written just after Gould began the Oral History and they are presumably a part of it. My thanks to Patricia J. Fanning of the Norwood Historical Society for sharing these letters with me.

21. Alfred Margulies, email to the author, June 1, 2015. Edward Shorter believes that the reason insane asylums got so crowded at the end of the nineteenth and

beginning of the twentieth centuries is the spread of syphilis. Shorter, *A History of Psychiatry: From the Era of the Asylum to the Age of Prozac* (New York: John Wiley & Sons, 1997), 53–59. After symptoms appeared, general paresis of the insane was fatal, until, during the First World War, it was discovered that it could be treated by inducing a fever. Syphilitic patients were then injected with the blood of patients suffering from malaria. In the 1940s, penicillin replaced inoculation with malaria as the preferred treatment. Ibid., 192–96. See also Elizabeth Lunbeck, *The Psychiatric Persuasion: Knowledge, Gender and Power in Modern America* (Princeton, NJ: Princeton University Press, 1994), 49–54. Locating an organic cause for insanity was revolutionary; it made psychiatry modern. "Syphilis is in a sense the making of psychiatry," the head of a psychiatric hospital in Boston said (quoted ibid.,50).

22. "This would indicate, perhaps, a commonness of the practice." Gould to Davenport, December 9, 1915, Davenport Papers.

23. Jerre Mangione, *An Ethnic at Large: A Memoir of America in the Thirties and Forties* (Syracuse, NY: Syracuse University Press, 1978), 110.

24. Gould to Davenport, December 24, 1915, and see also Davenport to Gould, January 7, 1916, Davenport Papers.

25. Gould to Davenport, December 9, 1915, Davenport Papers.

26. Gould's work was under the supervision of University of Minnesota anthropologist Albert Ernest Jenks. Davenport to Gould, September 14, 1915. And see Jenks, *Indian-White Amalgamation: An Anthropometric Study* (Minneapolis: Bulletin of the University of Minnesota, 1916), v–vi. In the end, Gould's work was too slow for Jenks's purposes, as Gould reported to the Eugenics Record Office in

November 1915: "my work will be done too late to be of any use in Prof. Jenk's [sic] law cases."

27. Gould to Hurlbut, October 28, 1915, from Elbo-woods, North Dakota: "I am to live with an Indian family, and will be in a village where there are only three other white people. During this time I should like to have a Harvard catalogue to pore over, and see if I cannot find some half course that can be taken by correspondence. . . . I am very anxious to get my degree, as there is a possibility of my getting a scholarship at the University of Minnesota, where Prof. A.E. Jenks is making some studies of racial amalgamation."

28. Gould to Hurlbut, January 14, 1916; and see Hurlbut to Professor Wiener (who taught Tolstoy), January 21, 1916, Gould Harvard Files.

29. Gould to Hurlbut, April 2, 1915, Gould Harvard Files.

30. Gould, review of *America's Greatest Problem*, by R. W. Shufeldt, *Survey*, November 27, 1915, 216; Gould, review of *The Education of the Negro Prior to 1861*, by Carter G. Woodson, *Survey*, January 29, 1916, 521–22.

31. "Certain of the Indian's problems are the same as those which beset the Negro." Gould to Du Bois, February 27, 1916, Du Bois Papers.

32. "Joseph Gould, '15, having completed his assignment among the Dakota Indians has been moving eastward by easy stages during the past month. On May 12 and 15 he spoke at Howard University, Washington, D. C., on 'America not a Melting Pot' and on 'Race Prejudice.' On May 26 he dropped into the 'Office' for a brief visit. He will remain for a time at his home in Norwood. Mass." *Eugenical News*, June 1916.

33. Earnest Albert Hooton, *Up from the Ape* (New York: Macmillan, 1937), 396–97, 501–2, 588–89, 594. This

is what Hooton wrote in 1937; he may have had different ideas in 1916, when he was teaching Gould. Still, his convictions are very strong, and it's hard to imagine that they represent a reversal. He was, for instance, quite vociferous in his opposition to IQ tests, which he said ought to be called "environment tests."

34. Gould, review of *The Institutional Care of the Insane in the United States and Canada, Volume III*, by Henry M. Hurd, *Survey*, January 27, 1917, 497–98: "Especially encouraging is the exposure of evil conditions that formerly existed at the Manhattan State Hospital, and the present development of this same institution."

CHAPTER 5

1. Mitchell, "Joe Gould's Secret."
2. Gould to Mitchell, January 13, 1946, Mitchell Papers, Box 9.1. "His quotations of me are rather inaccurate," Gould complained in a letter to the editor, *Harvard Crimson*, May 11, 1945.
3. Mitchell, interview with Colleen Chassan, August 3, 1959, Mitchell Papers, Box 9.1.
4. Gould to Mumford, July 1943, Mumford Papers, Box 23, Folder 1906.
5. Gould to Mitchell, July 30, 1945, Mitchell Papers, Box 9.1. The anthology, a collection of humor, was H. Allen Smith, compiler, *Desert Island Decameron* (New York: Doubleday, Doran & Co., 1945).
6. Diary entry for April 17, 1945, Gould Diaries.
7. On Mitchell's composite and invented characters like Mr. Flood of the Fulton Fish Market, the subject of two Reporter-at-Large pieces, and Cockeye Johnny Nikanov, the subject of Mitchell's 1942 profile "King of the Gypsies," see Thomas Kunkel, *Man*

in Profile: Joseph Mitchell of The New Yorker (New York: Random House, 2015). Kunkel quotes a letter Mitchell wrote in 1961. "Insofar as the principal character is concerned, the gypsy king himself, it is a work of the imagination," Mitchell wrote. "Cockeye Johnny Nikanov does not exist in real life, and never did." Kunkel argues that blurring the line between fact and fiction had been common in the magazine, especially during its early years and while under the editorship of Harold Ross, who died in 1951.

8. Gould, letter to the editor, *Harvard Crimson*, May 11, 1945.

9. Mitchell quoted in Kunkel, *Man in Profile*, 233.

10. Stanley Hyman to Joseph Mitchell, September 27, 1964, Mitchell Papers, Box 9.1. Hyman was a literary critic and the husband of Shirley Jackson. "Shirley adds her congratulations and love," he signed off.

11. Francis Bacon, "Of Truth," in *Essays* (London, 1597).

12. Mitchell's 1942 research notes, Mitchell Papers, Box 9.1.

13. Mitchell to G. A. Maclean, October 2, 1947, Mitchell Papers, Box 9.1.

14. Gould, "A Chapter from Joe Gould's Oral History: Art," *Exile*, November 1927, 116.

15. Mitchell, "Professor Sea Gull."

16. Gould, "Synopsis."

17. Diary entry for April 13, 1946, Gould Diaries.

18. Ben Hellman to Mitchell, September 25, 1964, Mitchell Papers, Box 10.1. The library, "contrary to my expectations, proved a poor place to work," Gould told Mitchell: it "reminded me that there were already more bks printed than any one person could hope to read." Mitchell's notes on Gould talking about the Oral History, 1942, Mitchell Papers, Box 9.1.

19. Mitchell, "Joe Gould's Secret."

20. Mitchell, typewritten note to himself while writing

the second profile, undated but ca. 1962, Mitchell Papers, Box 9.1.

21. Mitchell had held in his hands several different notebooks. In his notes from 1942, he lists their contents—they are essays, not "oral parts"—and indicates the dates the various sections were written, for example, 1921, 1923, etc. See Mitchell's notes on Gould and the Oral History, 1942, Mitchell Papers, Box 9.1. He writes, for instance, after reading one notebook: "typical ending of an entry in the O.H.: 'This is all that I will say about my theories of social position as I write these lines at 20 minutes of 10 in the evening of Monday, September 10, 1934, in the Lex. Ave. express uptown which is stopping at Moshulu Parkway station of the Lex. Ave. subway where I am being ragged (or nagged) by a loquacious drunk." Mitchell's discarded Gould interview notes from June 16, 1942, Mitchell Papers, Box 9.1. Mitchell also copied and typed the entirety of the "Tomato Habit" essay. Gould, "The Tomato Habit," typewritten by Mitchell, Mitchell Papers, Box 9.1.

22. Mitchell's miscellaneous research notes from 1942, Mitchell Papers, Box 9.1.

23. Mitchell's Norwood notes, July 24, 1959, Mitchell Papers, Box 9.1.

24. Carlo Sovello to Mitchell, October 19, 1964, Mitchell Papers, Box 9.1.

25. Richard A. Hitchcock to Mitchell, November 11, 1965, Mitchell Papers, Box 9.1. Gould mentioned his friendship with Hitchcock in a letter to Nino Frank, the editor of *Bifur*, March 1930, *Bifur* Archive, Box 1, Folder 13. He also mentions Hitchcock frequently in his diaries from the 1940s.

26. Mitchell to Richard A. Hitchcock, December 9, 1965, Mitchell Papers, Box 9.1.

27. Florence Lowe to Mitchell, November 16, 1964, and March 13, 1965, and Mitchell to Lowe, Decem-

ber 3, 1964, and February 25, 1965, Mitchell Papers, Box 9.1. Gould had first arrived in New York, in October 1916. Gould to Braithwaite, December 2, 1916, Braithwaite Collection, Box 8, Folder of Joseph F. Gould.

28. Joseph F. Gould, "Meo Tempore. Seventh Version. Volume II," unpublished manuscript, 1922, Mitchell Papers, Box 9.1.

29. A further description of the oral parts of the Oral History came from Ruth Mooney, who knew Gould well in the 1920s; she was married to the poet Lew Ney. Mooney wrote Mitchell, "Once Joe did read me a chapter of the Oral History which was really oral. He assembled in one place all he had ever heard people say about Alfred E. Smith. It was a collection of trivia without anything to recommend it by way of either historical sense of style. All that sticks in my memory is the story (told about Mrs. Smith and the wives of six previous politicians) that the Queen of Belgium had said, on a visit here, 'This is a wonderful city' and Mrs. Smith had replied 'You said a mouthful, Queen.' I was surprised to hear that there never was an Oral History but am sure that, if there had been, it would have been on this level." Ruth Mooney to Mitchell, March 11, 1964 [sic; corrected to 1965 by Mitchell], Mitchell Papers, Box 9.1. Lew Ney's real name was Luther Widen. He took the name "Lew Ney" (pronounced "looney") after he escaped from the Elgin Hospital for the Insane in 1916.

30. Gould, "Meo Tempore. Seventh Version. Volume II," 1922.

CHAPTER 6

1. A version of Gould's essay on insanity appeared in *Pagany* in 1931. But the version quoted here is the manuscript: "Meo Tempore. Seventh Version. Volume II," 1922, in the Joseph Mitchell Papers.

2. Regarding New York, "I describe clinics at the three largest insane asylums in the state which I attended while a student of the Eugenics Record Office." Gould, "Synopsis," 7.

3. Gregory described the oral chapters of the history this way: "In general the history is a record of nearly everything that Mr. Gould has heard (hence 'oral'), seen or thought during his fifteen years of wandering. It includes his autobiography and the biographies of a few of his friends, data upon the insane asylums at Central Islip and King's Park, notations scrawled on the walls of public latrines, reminiscences of a New England childhood, gossip overheard in Greenwich Village and Harlem, and rumors concerning public men that are retailed in and out of New York City, New England and Nova Scotia." Horace Gregory, "Pepys on the Bowery," *New Republic*, April 15, 1931.

4. Gould, "Meo Tempore. Seventh Version. Volume II," 1922.

5. Gould, "My Life," 3.

6. Ibid., 8.

7. Gould to Braithwaite, December 2, 1916, Braithwaite Collection, Box 8, Folder of Joseph F. Gould.

8. "If you wish you might add the information that I received a special mention in trying for the Menorah prize." Gould to Hurlbut, November 8, 1918, Gould Harvard Files. The Menorah Prize was given for "the best essay by an undergraduate on a subject concerning the history and achievements of the Jewish people." The prize was first awarded in 1908. Intercollegiate Menorah Association, *The Menorah*

Movement for the Study and Advancement of Jewish Culture and Ideals: History, Purposes, Activities (Ann Arbor, MI: Intercollegiate Menorah Association, 1914), 101–3.

9. "I am at present on the staff of the Evening Mail, as three attempts to volunteer for military service were unsuccessful." Gould to Hurlbut, November 8, 1918, Gould Harvard Files. On his draft card, in 1917, Gould listed his occupation as "Journalist" and his employer as the Leslie Company. Joseph Ferdinand Gould, Registration Card, *U.S., World War I Draft Registration Cards, 1917–1918* (Provo, UT: Ancestry .com Operations Inc., 2005).

10. Gould, "A Chapter from Joe Gould's Oral History: Art," *Exile*, November 1927, 113.

11. Clarke Storer Gould died on March 28, 1919, of septicemia. "Memorial to Clarke Storer Gould, M.D.," *Boston Medical and Surgical Journal* 180 (1919): 542–43; Gould, "My Life," 4.

12. Gould to Maclean, March 15, 1921, Mitchell Papers, Box 9.1.

13. Gould to Braithwaite, May 22, 1922, Braithwaite Papers, 428. And see Gould to Pound, January 4, 1928, Pound Papers, Box 19, Folder 861.

14. Gould to Braithwaite, April 1, 1922, Braithwaite Papers, 428.

15. Gould to Maclean, July 7, 1921, Mitchell Papers, Box 9.1.

16. Gould to Maclean, 1923, Mitchell Papers, Box 9.1.

17. The earliest biographical treatment is Eric Walrond, "Florida Girl Shows Amazing Gift for Sculpture," *Negro World*, December 16, 1922, though it contains some factual errors. Other early accounts are Augusta Savage, "An Autobiography," *Crisis*, August 1929; and Savage, Federal Arts Commission interview at her studio, June 20, 1935, Savage Papers, Box 1, Folder 2. Savage's first husband was named

John Moore. A brief biographical treatment with reproductions of some of Savage's work is in Gary A. Reynolds and Beryl J. Wright, *Against the Odds: African-American Artists and the Harmon Foundation* (Newark, NJ: Newark Museum, 1989), 251–54. See also Unpublished Biography of Augusta Savage, November 20, 1928, Rosenwald Archives, Box 445, Folder 12. On the illiteracy of Savage's mother, see Millen Brand's diary entry for April 9, 1935, Journals, 1919–1943, Brand Papers, Box 76.

18. Du Bois, "The Technique of Race Prejudice," *Crisis* 26 (August 1923): 152–54. See also Hugh Samson to Clyde J. Hart Jr., September 24, 1989, Hugh Samson Letters, Smithsonian Archives of American Art. And see, for example, "I do so want him to have one of my sister Irene's old southern cooked dinners." Savage to Countee Cullen, no date, Cullen Papers. Cullen was also an associate of Gould's. In 1932, Gould listed Cullen among the sponsors of his Oral History Society. See Gould to Joseph Freeman, December 31, 1932, Joseph Freeman Collection, Box 25, Folder 10, Hoover Institution Archives. (Other sponsors included Malcolm Cowley, E. E. Cummings, Horace Gregory, and Pauline Leader.)

19. "C'est une jeune femme mince, à la voix extraordinairement douce, d'une simplicité qui la rend immédiatement sympathique," a reporter wrote about Savage when she was later studying in Paris. Paulette Nardal, "Une Femme Sculpteur Noire," *La Dépêche Africaine*, August–September 1930, 4.

20. Gould, "My Life," 5.

21. Savage, Application Form, May 17, 1929, Rosenwald Archives, Box 445, Folder 12.

22. "Poet's Evening," *New York Age*, March 24, 1923.

23. Robert Lincoln Poston, "When You Meet a Member of the Ku Klux Klan" (1921), in *African Fundamentalism: A Cultural Anthology of Garvey's Harlem Renais-*

sance, ed. Tony Martin (Dover, MA: The Majority Press, 1991), 169.

24. "Color Line Drawn by Americans," *New York Amsterdam News*, April 25, 1923.

25. "Miss Augusta Savage," unpublished biography, November 20, 1928, Rosenwald Archives, Box 445, Folder 12.

26. "Miss Savage Tells Story at Lyceum," *New York Amsterdam News*, May 16, 1923.

27. Quoted in Romare Bearden and Harry Henderson, *Six Black Masters of American Art* (New York: Doubleday & Co., 1972), 76–98. And see Du Bois, "The Technique of Race Prejudice."

28. "Appeal Artists' Race Ban," *New York Times*, May 11, 1923.

29. For more on Savage, see Romare Bearden and Harry Henderson, *A History of African American Artists: From 1792 to the Present* (New York: Pantheon, 1993), 168–80; Denise Ellaine Hinnant, "Sculptor Augusta Savage: Her Art, Progressive Influences, and African-American Representation" (M.A. thesis, University of Louisville, 1991); and Theresa Leininger-Miller, *New Negro Artists in Paris: African American Painters and Sculptors in the City of Light, 1922–1934* (New Brunswick, NJ: Rutgers University Press, 2001).

30. Hinnant, "Sculptor Augusta Savage," 110.

31. Cummings was terribly fond of this poem and set it in dozens of different ways before settling on its final form. See E. E. Cummings, "as joe gould says in," Cummings Papers, Additional I, folders 50 and 51, and also Cummings to Qualey, April 16, 1955, Cummings and Qualey Papers, Box 2, Folder 30.

32. A typescript edition with Cummings's original drawings is E. E. Cummings, *The Enormous Room* (1922; New York: Liveright, 2014), with an introduction by Susan Cheever. Matthew Josephson writes

that Cummings delighted in humiliating Gould, quite cruelly. This doesn't strike me as impossible, but I haven't seen anyone else describe it this way. Josephson and Gould hated each other. Matthew Josephson, *Life Among the Surrealists: A Memoir* (New York: Holt, Rinehart & Winston, 1962), 90–93, 272–73; see also 384–85.

33. Gould, "Social Position," *Broom* 5 (October 1923): 147–49.

34. For example, "I was much less aware than I later became of the ph.d. candidate's passion for footnotes and sources, but I knew a little about it, and I thought the book was, in effect, a parody, and a parody also of the H.G. Wells Outline of History and the Hendrik Willem Van Loon Story of Mankind, with Joe patiently tracing the history of the universe from its gaseous beginnings and documents each stage of the way by something somebody had told him." Bob Cantwell to Mitchell, September 27, 1964, Mitchell Papers, Box 10.1. Robert Cantwell was a novelist and critic whose first novel, *Laugh and Lie Down*, was published in 1931. His criticism appeared in *The New Republic*; Cowley was his editor. See Cowley, *The Dream of the Golden Mountains: Remembering the 1930s* (New York: Viking, 1980), 126–27 and 262–63; and T. V. Reed, *Robert Cantwell and the Literary Left: A Northwest Writer Reworks American Fiction* (Seattle: University of Washington Press, 2014).

35. Norman, "Joe Gould Writes History as He Hears It."

36. Edward Nagel and Slater Brown, "Joseph Gould: The Man," *Broom* 5 (October 1923): 145–46, with a sketch by Joseph Stella.

37. See Hugh Kenner, *The Pound Era* (Berkeley: University of California Press, 1971); and Louis Menand, "The Pound Error," *New Yorker*, June 9, 2008.

38. William Butler Yeats, "Rapallo" (March and April 1928), in *A Vision* (London: Macmillan, 1937), 5–6.

39. Pound, "Dr Williams' Position," *Dial*, November 1928, 396.

40. Joseph J. Boris, ed., *Who's Who in Colored America: A Biographical Dictionary of Notable Living Persons of Negro Descent in America*, vol. 1 (New York: Phillis Wheatley Publishing Co., 1927). The editor in chief was Roscoe Conkling Bruce. The board of editors included Du Bois, Alain Locke, and James Weldon Johnson. See the letterhead in Helen L. Watts, Associate Editor, Phillis Wheatley Publishing Co., to Du Bois, February 16, 1926, Du Bois Papers.

41. Gould to Williams, January 16, 1925, Williams Papers, Box 7, Folder 243.

42. Gould to Pound, February 15, 1930, Pound Papers, Box 19, Folder 861, in which he also says, "I am tremendously pleased and obliged that you had my manuscript typed." On Pound having Gould's notebooks typed, see also Pound to Williams, November 5, 1929: "I at least sent off some of Gould's stuff to a London typist." *Pound/Williams*, 99. And: "You will be pleased to hear that Ezra Pound has typed some of my manuscript and has sent it to Hound and Horn. I asked him to send it to Bijur the French quarterly which had asked for some of it but quite characteristically he sent it elsewhere. He said the Hound and Horn paid better. If that magazine does take it, it will be very good luck for me. Other magazines watch the Hound and Horn as well as publishers of books." Gould to Lachaise, February 1930, Lachaise Collection, Box 1. One trail in the search for the lost Oral History leads to the offices of *Hound & Horn*. In March 1930, Gould wrote to the novelist Nino Frank, the editor of *Bifur*, "None of my manuscript on this side of the ocean has been typed. I wrote Edward O'Brien and Ezra Pound who had some of it. O'Brien said he had sent it all to Ezra Pound. Pound

wrote me and said that he had got quite a batch of my manuscript typed. He had sent it to Hound and Horn. This magazine is edited by a group of Harvard students. Apparently they are not very businesslike. I wrote to them and did not receive a reply. I do not know which chapters they have." *Bifur* Archive, Box 1, Folder 13.

43. Gould to Mark Antony De Wolfe Howe, December 5, 1927, Mark Antony De Wolfe Howe Additional Papers, Houghton Library, MS Am 524, 550.

44. Gould, "A Chapter from Joe Gould's Oral History: Art," *Exile*, November 1927, 112–16; quotation from 113–14.

45. On the Baltimore exhibit, see Hope Finkelstein, "Augusta Savage: Sculpting the African-American Identity" (M.A. thesis, City University of New York, 1990), 16.

46. Du Bois, "Criteria of Negro Art," *Crisis* 32, no. 6 (October 1927): 290–97. Lynn Igoe and James Moody, *250 Years of Afro-American Art: Annotated Bibliography* (New York: R. R. Bowker, 1981), 294, where they identify Savage as the subject of Du Bois's remarks.

47. Du Bois to Savage, April 20, 1926; Du Bois to Irene Di Robilant, April 20, 1926; and Savage to Du Bois, May 26, 1926, Du Bois Papers.

48. Leininger-Miller, *New Negro Artists in Paris*, 176. And see "Harlem Soap Sculptors Win Praise," *Chicago Defender*, February 2, 1929.

49. Hinnant, "Sculptor Augusta Savage," 64; Leininger-Miller, *New Negro Artists in Paris*, 176–77.

50. See, for example, Savage to West, August 19, 1935, West Papers, Box 2, Folder 13.

51. Savage to Cullen, February 27, 1931, Cullen Papers. On Cullen, see the introduction by Major Jackson to Countee Cullen, *Collected Poems* (New York: Library of America, 2013).

52. Richard Bruce Nugent, "Smoke, Lilies and Jade," here as quoted in Hinnant, "Sculptor Augusta Savage," 50. For more on Savage's presence and influence in Harlem, see the oral history interview with Norman Lewis, July 14, 1968, Archives of American Art, Smithsonian Institution.

53. So far as I have been able to discover, not one word about their relationship ever made it into print. The sole mention I have found does not provide Savage's name. In a history of the Federal Writers' Project, Jerre Mangione alluded to Gould's obsession with "a black sculptress." Mangione wrote:

> Behind this benign façade bubbled a volcano of bad temper which was apt to erupt when anyone crossed him. One of his victims, a black sculptress who had apparently spurned his advances, he attacked with a barrage of obscene phone calls and letters. When the novelist Millen Brand, a friend of the sculptress, tried to make him desist, Gould began bombarding him and his wife with obscene letters. Brand finally felt compelled to complain to the police, who issued a warrant for his arrest. As soon as the warrant was served Gould got in touch with Brand and begged him to drop the charge, confessing he had been similarly served on two other occasions; another time would mean going to jail. A kindly man, Brand agreed to withdraw the charge but not before making it clear that one more letter or phone call either to his family or to the sculptress would land him in jail.

> Jerre Mangione, *The Dream and the Deal: The Federal Writers' Project, 1935–1943* (Philadelphia: University of Pennsylvania Press, 1983), 180–81. Mangione's citation is to an interview with Millen Brand. My thanks to Phillip Koyoumjian, who looked for

Mangione's interview with Brand among Mangione's papers at the University of Rochester; it is not there.

54. Gould to Cummings, September 20, 1926, Cummings Papers, Additional I, Folder 338.

55. Morris R. Werner to Mitchell, September 25, 1964, Mitchell Papers, Box 10.1.

56. Gould to Pound, May 27, 1927, Pound Papers, Box 19, Folder 861. Gould also described his conflict with Liveright in 1929, in a letter to Nino Frank, December 1929, *Bifur* Archive, Box 1, Folder 13.

57. Gould to Pound, March 1928 and January 1931, Pound Papers, Box 19, Folder 861. At the time, Zukofsky was serving as guest editor of *Poetry*.

58. Werner to Mitchell, September 25, 1964, Mitchell Papers, Box 10.1.

59. "He had his say, which was considerable, about the book, the author, and the subject, and there for him the matter ended." Entry for Friday, February 15, 1924, in Burton Rascoe, *A Bookman's Daybook* (New York: Horace Liveright, 1929), 206. A note with this typed on it is in Mitchell Papers, Box 9.1.

60. Gould to Moore, February 25, 1926, *Dial* Papers, Box 2, Folder 80. Gould hated Scofield: "The gulf which yawns and yawns and yawns between the bumptious pretenses of the Dial and its slight performance is based upon the incongruity of a shoddy-miller trying to run a magazine."

61. See Pound to Zukofsky, August 12, 1928, *Pound/Zukofsky*, 12, 15. Zukofsky looked out for Gould. See Zukofsky to Pound, December 5 and December 12–28, 1928, *Pound/Zukofsky*, 22–23.

62. Moore made this selection after reading Gould's notebooks. Moore to Gould, December 4, 1928, *Dial* Papers, Box 2, Folder 80.

63. He didn't mind her edits. "I consented readily," he explained to Pound, "because I think of my book as substance rather than form. She was typically quietly

and secretly afraid that she was bursting my literary conscience. I told her not to worry that one could do things to a whale without hurting it which one could not do to a humming bird. I meant, of course, merely that my work should be judged according to scale as one judges Froissart or Balzac and not that in literary merit had the jeweled cadence of a humming bird. I envy those who are able to publish every sentence but I have taken in too much history to be able to do this." Gould to Moore, December 12, 1928, *Dial* Papers, Box 2, Folder 80; Gould to Pound, December 1928, Pound Papers, Box 19, Folder 861.

64. Gould to Moore, December 28, 1928, *Dial* Papers, Box 2, Folder 80.

65. Moore also tried to get Gould to submit reviews, without success. Moore to Gould, December 17, 1928, *Dial* Papers, Box 2, Folder 80.

66. Gould, "From Joe Gould's Oral History: Marriage," *Dial*, April 1929, 319–21.

67. Gould refers to this in a letter to Brand, September 7, 1934, Brand Papers, uncataloged Box 1, Gould folder.

CHAPTER 7

1. Gould, "My Life," 7.

2. Gould to Pound, December 1928, Pound Papers, Box 19, Folder 861.

3. Gould to Pound, May 6, 1933, Pound Papers, Box 19, Folder 861.

4. Macdonald said that Gould began writing the first version of the Oral History on October 1, 1914 (that would be right after he got back to Norwood from the Dakotas). "He started it all over again on January 1, 1915, and has since made a fresh start every January first since." Macdonald, Statement on Joe

Gould, unpublished eleven-page typewritten essay, Macdonald Papers, Box 78, Folder 142.

5. Savage to Arthur Schomburg, January 1935, quoted in Hope Finkelstein, "Augusta Savage: Sculpting the African-American Identity" (M.A. thesis, City University of New York, 1990), 29–30. "By 1934 Augusta Savage was considered the most influential artist in Harlem." Deirdre L. Bibby, foreword to *Augusta Savage and the Arts Schools of Harlem* (New York: Schomburg Center for Research in Black Culture, 1988), 8. An indication of Savage's prominence in the Harlem arts movement: "Among the Negro artists of Harlem are Augusta Savage, Aaron Douglas, Richmond Barthe, Charles Alston, E. Sims Campbell, Vertis Hayes, Bruce Nugent, Henry W. Barnham, Sara Murrell, Romare Beardon, Robert Savon Pious, and Beauford Delaney. Of these Aaron Douglas, painter and mural artist, Richmond Barthe, sculptor, Augusta Savage, sculptress, and E. Sims Campbell, painter and cartoonist, are the most prominent." Federal Writers' Project, *New York Panorama: A Comprehensive View of the Metropolis* (New York: Random House, 1938), 143. See also "Sculptress of the Negro People," *Daily Worker*, December 24, 1937.

6. T. R. Poston, "Augusta Savage," *Metropolitan*, January 1935. And see Finkelstein, "Augusta Savage," chapter 2.

7. On the shoe-polish formula, see Hugh Samson to Clyde J. Hart Jr., September 24, 1989, Hugh Samson Letters, Smithsonian Archives of American Art.

8. For example: "I found several people who knew me. They kept buying me drinks. One was a Mrs. White who looked like [deliberate blank space] the colored sculptress." Diary entry for October 8, 1945. I entertained the possibility that Gould meant Selma Burke, another African American sculptor he knew.

But when Gould writes about Burke, he uses her name; see his diary entry for July 20, 1946, Gould Diaries.

9. Undated typewritten excerpt from Joe Gould's Oral History, Brand Papers, uncataloged Box 1, Gould folder.

10. Mitchell's interview notes with Gould, 1942, Mitchell Papers, Box 9.1.

11. Brand to Mitchell, October 3, 1964, Mitchell Papers, Box 9.1.

12. Brand to Mitchell, October 3, 1964, Mitchell Papers, Box 9.1.

13. Brand and Leader married on November 10, 1931: Millen Brand, Journal 1930–31, Brand Papers, Box 76.

14. Pauline Leader, *And No Birds Sing* (New York: Vanguard, 1931), 82, 153, 174–89, and 214.

15. Gould, "My Life," 8.

16. Pauline Leader, "Two Poems," *Poetry* 31 (1928): 256–57; and "Poem to Emily Dickinson," *Poetry* 36 (1930): 85.

17. Horace Gregory, "Hard, Bitter and Courageous," *New York Herald Tribune*, June 28, 1931.

18. Brand, *The Outward Room* (1937; New York: New York Review Books, 2010), afterword by Peter Cameron.

19. American psychiatry and psychoanalysis lagged behind their European counterparts, and, in any case, the field of psychiatry had been more or less in crisis since about 1900, when, as Edward Shorter argues, "psychiatry had reached a dead end. Its practitioners were for the most part in asylums, and asylums had become mainly warehouses in which any hope of therapy was illusory." Edward Shorter, *A History of Psychiatry: From the Era of the Asylum to the Age of Prozac* (New York: John Wiley & Sons, 1997), 65. In Europe, the movement then turned to biology; this happened more slowly in the United States (ibid., chapter 3).

20. David J. Rothman calls this "the decline from reha-
    bilitation to custodianship." Rothman, *The Discovery
    of the Asylum: Social Order and Disorder in the New
    Republic* (Boston: Little, Brown, 1990), 239. For more
    on the displacement of the asylum with the mental
    hospital, see Elizabeth Lunbeck, *The Psychiatric
    Persuasion: Knowledge, Gender, and Power in Mod-
    ern America* (Princeton, NJ: Princeton University
    Press, 1994), 22; on the role of routine, see 163–65.
    As Shorter writes, the first asylum in the United
    States that simply gave up the pretense that anyone
    would ever be cured was the Willard State Hospi-
    tal, founded in 1869. Shorter, *History of Psychiatry*,
    46. Shorter calls the rise in numbers "the great
    nineteenth-century lockup" (48).

21. *The Outward Room* was a critical sensation and also
    sold more than half a million copies. See the after-
    word by Peter Cameron, 234–37; quotation from 42.
    For more about Brand, see his obituary: Eric Pace,
    "Millen Brand, Writer and Editor Known for Works
    on Psychiatry," *New York Times*, March 22, 1980.
    Brand had a full draft of the novel by 1933, which
    is right after his encounter with Gould over Sav-
    age. That year, he asked a psychiatrist to review the
    manuscript and received extensive feedback. See the
    letters of Louis J. Bragman, M.D., to Brand, Brand
    Papers, Box 1.

22. Brand to Jerre Mangione, May 4, 1965, Brand
    Papers, Box D.

23. Brand to Mitchell, October 3, 1964, Mitchell Papers,
    Box 9.1.

24. Brand to Mitchell, October 10, 1964, Mitchell
    Papers, Box 9.1.

25. George Arthur to Savage, May 28, 1930, Rosenwald
    Archives, Box 445, Folder 12.

26. Cullen to West, October 10, 1929, and July 3, 1931,
    West Papers, Box 2, Folder 7; Du Bois to Cullen,
    telegram, 1929, Du Bois Papers.

27. Gould, "My Life," 9.
28. Savage to George Arthur, June 15, 1930, Rosenwald Archives, Box 445, Folder 12.
29. Cummings quotes this as one of Gould's sayings in Cummings to Qualey, February 12, 1945, Cummings and Qualey Papers, Box 1, Folder 17.
30. "Augusta Savage Gives Her Views on Negro Art," *Pittsburgh Courtier*, September 26, 1936.
31. Savage to Du Bois, May 26, 1926, Du Bois Papers.
32. See especially Paulette Nardal, "Une Femme Sculpteur Noire," *La Dépêche Africaine*, August–September 1930, 4. On the general question of the loss and neglect of Savage's work, and her vanishing from history, see also Finkelstein, "Augusta Savage," 1.
33. "Young Sculptress Defies Adversity," *New Journal and Guide*, October 19, 1929. Du Bois also made various introductions for her there, etc. See, for example, Du Bois to Henry O. Tanner, August 27, 1929, Du Bois Papers. On Savage in Paris, see also Theresa Leininger-Miller, "'Heads of Thought and Reflection': Busts of African Warriors by Nancy Elizabeth Prophet and Augusta Savage, African American Sculptors in Paris, 1922–1934," in *Out of Context: American Artists Abroad*, ed. Laura Felleman Fattal and Carol Salus (Westport, CT: Praeger, 2004), 93–111; Krista A. Thompson, "Preoccupied with Haiti: The Dream of Diaspora in African American Art, 1915–1942," *American Art* 21, no. 3 (Fall 2007): 74–97; and Augusta Savage, *Mourning Victory*, ca. 1930, Special Collections, Fisk Library.
34. Mitchell's interview notes with Gould, 1942, Mitchell Papers, Box 9.1.
35. Gould to Williams, August 1929, Pound Papers, Box 19, Folder 861.
36. Mitchell later entertained this possibility. About 1959, when he was typing up a set of Gould interview notes from June 16, 1942, which he marked as "saved from several pages that I discarded," he

wrote this note to himself: "possibility that during his disappearance from the Village ref to in the profile ['Professor Sea Gull'] he was in Bellevue or some other hospital." Mitchell, discarded Gould interview notes, June 16, 1942, Mitchell Papers, Box 9.1.

CHAPTER 8

1. "One of the chapters I will read from the magnum opus is the Proud Man and the Colored Singer." Gould to Williams, August 1929, Pound Papers, Box 19, Folder 861.
2. Gould, "The Proud Man and the Colored Singer," originally written in 1929, Macdonald Papers. Gould notes that a version of the story was published in the *Greenwich Villager* in September 1933.
3. Gardiner Reminiscences, 43–44.
4. Cummings to Pound, March 1, 1930, *Pound/Cummings*, 18.
5. Wilson was *The New Republic*'s literary editor. For more on Cowley's role at the magazine, see his autobiography, *The Dream of the Golden Mountains: Remembering the 1930s* (New York: Viking, 1964).
6. Contributors, *New Republic*, October 1, 1930, 188.
7. He also got into a fight there. "I was asked to sign the New Republic manifesto against humanism. I refused. I said I had to devote so much time and energy to my own work that I had no time for religious controversy." Gould to Pound, April 10, 1930, Pound Papers, Box 7, Folder 169. Gould's reviews are for the most part sensible and lively. Here are some from this period of lucidity: "Sound and Fury," *New Republic*, June 4, 1930; "The Great Spirit," *New Republic*, August 20, 1930; and review of *Power for Profit*, by Robert Collyer Washburn, *New Republic*, October 1, 1930.

8. Gould, "Synopsis," 5.
9. Diary entries for May 6, July 13, August 2, and September 3, 1945, Gould Diaries.
10. Gould, "Freedom," *Pagany*, 1931, 97.
11. Mitchell's interview with Horace Gregory, typewritten notes, 1942, Mitchell Papers, Box 9.1. Wilson missed what came next: he left New York at the end of 1930 to travel the country, doing the reporting that lies behind *American Jitters* (1932). In 1927, for Lew Ney's National Poetry Exhibition, Gould wrote a poem about a woman taking a man to court for assault. It is called "Chivalry":

> It was only force of habit
> That made the half-wit nasty in the Black Rabbit.
> He said, "With many strange contortions,
> That girl has had twenty-one abortions,"
> And so Lew Ney the gentile parfaite tonight,
> Was hauled to court by Peggy White.
> The character witness was Emil Luft,
> So the Justice thought he was being spoofed.
> He said "We won't let this case pester us,
> You can't do in New York, what you do in Texas."

Graphic Arts Collection, Firestone Library, Princeton University. On Ney and the National Poetry Exhibition, see Julie Mellby, "The True and Honest Story of Lew Ney, Greenwich Village Printer," *Princeton University Library Chronicle* 75 (2013): 65–96.
12. Werner to Mitchell, September 25, 1964, Mitchell Papers, Box 10.1. Gould writes about Werner a lot in his diaries for 1943–1947. And see, for example, "I usually take breakfast with M.J. Werner once a week." Gould to Cummings, August 23, 1943, Cummings Papers, Folder 490.
13. Gould to Pound, January 1931, recalling the events of the spring of 1930, Pound Papers, Box 19, Folder 861.

14. Horace Gregory, "Pepys on the Bowery," *New Republic*, April 15, 1931.

15. Mitchell's interview with Gregory, typewritten notes, 1942, Mitchell Papers, Box 9.1. The publication of Gregory's article also led to Gould announcing, once again, his plans to found an Oral History Association. See, for example, "Lachaise was very pleased with the article on me. It seems to me that now is the time to try and arouse interest in what I am doing. I am therefore forming an Oral Historical Society." Gould to Edmund Wilson, May 26, 1931, Wilson Papers, Box 30, Folder 784.

16. "Where Poems Are Sold for Sandwiches," *Dallas Morning News*, September 27, 1931.

17. Gould first raised the possibility of applying for a Guggenheim Fellowship in a letter to Henry Allen Moe, October 15, 1931, Gould Guggenheim Files, in which he explained that he had earlier been reticent, because "it happens that my family were among the small investors who were hurt in the amassing of the Guggenheim fortune" but that the response to his work—presumably through the Gregory article—had changed his mind: "I am surprised at the number of people who are interested in my work." He then began writing to his possible recommenders. "You may be surprised to hear that I am trying to make friends of the Mammon of Unrighteousness," he wrote to Pound. "I am applying for a Guggenheim Fellowship to go to Geneva to collect material for my oral history. If I get this it will enable me to make contacts which should sell my book for me." Gould to Pound, October 22, 1931, Pound Papers, Box 19, Folder 861. This was right around when *Pagany* published two more chapters of the Oral History. Joe Gould, "Me Tempore: A Selection from Joe Gould's Oral History," *Pagany* 2 (1931): 96–99. The selections are two short essays, "I. Insanity," and "II. Freedom."

18. Gould, "Synopsis," and Gould, fellowship application, Gould Guggenheim Files, 1932. And see André Bernard, email to the author, April 17, 2015.

19. Gould to Pound, October 27, 1931, Pound Papers, Box 19, Folder 861.

20. Gould, fellowship application, November 30, 1931, and Moe to Gould, December 1, 1931, Gould Guggenheim Files. The deadline was November 30; Gould's application did not arrive in Moe's office until December 1.

21. Gould to Moe, December 17, 1931, Gould Guggenheim Files.

22. See, for example, Gould to Moe, August 9, 1932, Gould Guggenheim Files.

23. Gould wrote contemptuously about Cowley. See, for example, Gould to Pound, December 22, 1932, Pound Papers, Box 19, Folder 861; and Gould to "Dear Comrade," November 7, 1932, Cowley Papers, Box 106, Folder 5000.

24. Gould complained, "I knew the authors and helped them in their work in Harlem. In my junior year at Harvard I took courses in anthropology normally open only to undergraduates. Mr. Cowley's knowledge of the subject is derived from the Daily Worker." Gould to George Soule, August 12, 1934, Cowley Papers, Box 106, Folder 5000. The Herskovitses' book was called *Rebel Destiny;* Cowley reviewed it in *The New Republic* ("Primitive Peoples," June 20, 1934).

25. Gould to Brand, undated but 1934, Brand Papers, uncataloged papers, Box 1, Gould folder.

26. Gould, "Warpath," *New Republic*, December 12, 1934.

27. Gould, "Belated May Day Poem," *New Republic*, May 13, 1936.

28. "Joe Gould . . . got a dollar every Wednesday. . . . Once or twice I tried giving him a book for review, but that was a failed experiment; I suspected that he had sold the books before reading them." But then

Otis Ferguson, the head of the book department, objected:

> Otis laid down an edict: no weekly dollar except when Joe submitted something short for the correspondence page. The following Wednesday Joe appeared with a sheet torn from one of his notebooks. "Now you can give me my dollar," he said as he passed it over. The sheet contained a couplet which Otis recited from memory:

> Dear God, save Malcolm Cowley from harm,
> Or at least break his neck instead of his arm.

Cowley, *Dream of the Golden Mountains*, 261–62, 293. Gould's efforts in *The New Republic* during the latter part of the 1930s steadily declined in quality. See "Poet Among the Planets," *New Republic*, May 20, 1936; "Song of the Glass-Conscious Intellectuals," *New Republic*, June 3, 1936; "A Vote for Landon," *New Republic*, October 28, 1936; "Restless Life," *New Republic*, August 4, 1937; "Communism Is 20th Century Americanism," *New Republic*, September 7, 1938 (but in the letters section). "The Third-Class Mailbox," *New Republic*, October 3, 1939, which is simply a scrap, is introduced this way:

> Joe Gould, who is growing a beard again, brought into the office a follow-up on his poem ("Communism Is Twentieth Century Americanism") in which Earl Browder was found to have switched from borscht to clam chowder:

> Now Comrade Browder
> Lieks Wienerworscht
> Both in his chowder
> And in his borscht.

29. Gould to Moe, August 9, 1932, and September 12, 1932, Gould Guggenheim Files.

30. Gaston Lachaise, letter of recommendation for Gould, 1932, Gould Guggenheim Files.

31. Gould, review of *Scandinavian Immigrants in New York, 1630–1674*, by John Olaf Evjen, *Survey*, October 21, 1916, 71: "The problems of New York state are essentially an exaggerated form of the great American problem of keeping unity among various racial stocks, without crushing the initiative of any ethnic group."

32. John Olaf Evjen, letter of recommendation for Gould, 1932, Gould Guggenheim Files. Evjen had read the "Synopsis." He wrote, "The work he has outlined should prove a storehouse of fascinating material. It would have the charm of Well's History, of Durant's Philosophy, the works of Van Loon and of Ludwig. But I think Gould would exercise more restraint than any of these, and be more careful of scientific truth."

33. Gould to Moe, November 21, 1932, and Moe to Gould, August 13, 1932, Gould Guggenheim Files. Whatever manuscript Gould may ultimately have submitted—and it appears he did submit some unpublished material—was returned to him. On February 16, 1933, he signed a receipt acknowledging the return of all the materials he had submitted in support of his application. Gould Guggenheim Files.

34. Gould to Moe, August 28, 1932, Gould Guggenheim Files.

35. The only parts he had that were typed were the parts he'd sent to O'Brien nearly a decade before. Gould to Pound, October 25, 1932. And see Gould to Lincoln Kirstein of the *Hound & Horn*, from Central Hotel, January 7 and January 13, 1933, *Hound & Horn* Records, Box 2, Folder labeled Joe Gould.

36. Gould to Moe, November 21, 1932, Gould Guggenheim Files.

37. Gould, "Synopsis," 1–9.

38. Moe to Gould (letter of rejection), March 11, 1933, Gould Guggenheim Files; Gould to Edmund Brown, July 1934; February 4, April 1, May 5, and June 5, 1935, Brown Papers, Barrett Minor Box 10.

39. Pound to Williams, April 28, 1936, *Pound/Williams*, 180; Gould to Pound, November 1936, Pound Papers, Box 19, Folder 861.

CHAPTER 9

1. Gould to Cullen, November 28, 1931, Cullen Papers.

2. "Noted Sculptress Expects Distinct, but Not Different, Racial Art," *Pittsburgh Courier*, August 29, 1936.

3. Savage to George R. Arthur, October 19, 1931, Rosenwald Archives, Box 445, Folder 12.

4. On the Vanguard, see the entry for Savage in Carey D. Wintz and Paul Finkelman, eds., *Encyclopedia of the Harlem Renaissance* (New York: Routledge, 2004).

5. McKay and Savage were close. In 1934, McKay lived with her. See Lawrence Patrick Jackson, *The Indignant Generation: A Narrative History of African American Writers and Critics, 1934–1960* (Princeton, NJ: Princeton University Press, 2011), 68. On the FBI's Racial Division, see William J. Maxwell, *F.B. Eyes: How J. Edgar Hoover's Ghostreaders Framed African American Literature* (Princeton, NJ: Princeton University Press, 2015).

6. Gould does not have an FBI file. David M. Hardy, Record/Information Dissemination Section, Federal Bureau of Investigation, to the author, April 14, 2015.

7. A copy of Savage's FBI file, the result of a Freedom of Information Act request made by David Garrow

in the 1980s, is filed at the Schomburg Center in a manuscript collection called "Surveillance Files on African American Intellectuals and Activists Obtained from the FBI Archives via a Freedom of Information Act Request." The file has been massively redacted. Thirty-two pages were deleted in their entirety; most of the rest have only two or three words left legible. A document titled "The Communist Party; National Professional Organizations and Organizations of Professionals," dated October 13, 1936, includes the American Civil Liberties Union, the Association for the Study of Negro Life and History, and "The Vanguard (An association of Negro and white intellectuals for social study and protest)," which lists "Augusta Savage, Chairman." Her name also appears on a list, dated March 4, 1941, of American artists who were members of the American Artists Congress. A memo dated December 3, 1941, describes the activities of the American Artists Congress. An internal letter to Hoover states, "Files of this office reflect that in 1941 AUGUSTA SAVAGE was a member of the Artists Congress and on the mailing list of New York Conference for Inalienable Rights." An inter-office memo concerning Savage, addressed to Hoover, is dated April 10, 1951; its entire contents are redacted.

8. Gould to Savage, undated but 1934, Brand Papers, uncataloged Box 1, Gould folder.
9. Gould, "My Life," 9.
10. Alice Neel, *Joe Gould*, oil on canvas, 1933, on loan to the Tate Modern, London.
11. Phoebe Hoban, *Alice Neel: The Art of Not Sitting Pretty* (New York: St. Martin's, 2010), 94–97. As Hoban points out, Neel did not admire Mitchell's writing about Gould, saying that it "had an O. Henry ending," and that Mitchell was wrong to say the Oral History never existed. While research-

ing her biography of Neel, Hoban discovered four chapters of Gould's Oral History in Millen Brand's papers at Columbia, along with documents concerning Gould's relationship with Augusta Savage. In *Alice Neel*, Hoban mentions one of the chapters of Gould's Oral History (94), but she does not mention any of the Savage material. I didn't read Hoban's biography of Neel until after I had completed my own research. Hoban wrote to me after my essay, "Joe Gould's Teeth," appeared in *The New Yorker*. My thanks to her for pointing me to her work on Neel.

12. Gould to Leader, October 13, 1934, Brand Papers, uncataloged Box 1, Gould folder.

13. Gould, "My Life," 9.

14. See Romare Bearden and Harry Henderson, *A History of African-American Artists: From 1792 to the Present* (New York: Pantheon, 1993), 175–76.

15. Gould to Brand, undated, ca. December 1934, Brand Papers, uncataloged Box 1, Gould folder.

16. Brand to Mitchell, October 1964, Mitchell Papers, Box 9.1.

17. Gould to Brand, undated but 1934 and September 7 and 26, 1934, Brand Papers, uncataloged Box 1, Gould folder.

18. Gould to Brand, October 13 and September 7, 1934, Brand Papers, uncataloged Box 1, Gould folder.

19. Brand to Mitchell, October 10, 1964, Mitchell Papers, Box 9.1.

20. Brand to Mitchell, October 3 and 10, 1964, Mitchell Papers, Box 9.1.

21. Brand, note to the archivist, October 20, 1954, Brand Papers, uncataloged Box 1, Gould folder.

22. Gould to Leader, September 24, 1934, Brand Papers, uncataloged Box 1, Gould folder.

23. Gould to Jonathan Brand, January 8, 1935, Brand Papers, uncataloged Box 1, Gould folder.

24. Brand to Mitchell, October 3, 1964, Mitchell Papers, Box 9.1.
25. Brand to Mitchell, October 10, 1964, Mitchell Papers, Box 9.1.
26. Edward J. O'Brien, letter of recommendation for Gould, 1934, Gould Guggenheim Files.
27. Moe to Gould, March 14, 1935; Gould to Moe, February 20, 1936 (at the bottom of this letter, Moe has written "no!"); and Gould to Moe, no date, but marked as received April 21, 1939, Gould Guggenheim Files.
28. "Look, Joe, please don't sit on the upholstered furniture, sit on the woolen chairs," Marquie told Gould when he came to the gallery. "He didn't mind, he understood, he said that E.E. Cummings made him sit on the window case." Mitchell, interview notes with E. P. Marquie, May 1959, Mitchell Papers, Box 9.1.
29. Mitchell, interview notes with Erika Feist, June 24, 1959, Mitchell Papers, Box 9.1.
30. Gould to Edmund Brown, January 5, 1934:

> O'Brien thought I ought to delay my book until next fall. He said it would be built up more. He offered his assistant, but his principle [sic] idea was very flukey. He wants to sell me to the public as a sort of William Saroyan. He introduced me to Allan Seager, the editor of Vanity Fair. Seager saw some of my stuff. He said they could use oodles of it after my book is published. One of his suggestions was a "profile" in the New Yorker and another was that he could get me in the Vanity Fair Hall of Fame. Cowley thinks that Peggy Bacon may do a sketch of me for the New Republic and he could use his influence to get a profile of me published.

Brown Papers, Barrett Minor Box 10.
31. Pound to Cummings, April 28, 1935, *Pound/Cummings*, 65.

32. Although it apparently seemed as if they would: Cummings to Pound, "Bravo JoeGould—Esquire!!," May 1935, *Pound/Cummings*, 69.

33. Cummings to Pound, May 1935, *Pound/Cummings*, 73–74. Cummings's sister, Elizabeth Cummings Qualey, was a social worker in New York from 1926 to the summer of 1936. See Qualey, "Notes to assist in understanding letters from Estlin to Elizabeth," July 1965, Cummings and Qualey Papers, Box 1, Folder 1.

34. "God pity the women he fell in love with," Morris Werner wrote to Mitchell. "She came to me for advice when he kept bombarding her with letters and phone calls. I told her not to answer any of his letters and to make it clear to him sternly that he was not to bother her." Werner to Mitchell, September 25, 1964, Mitchell Papers, Box 9.1.

35. Richard A. Hitchcock to Mitchell, November 11, 1965, Mitchell Papers, Box 9.1.

36. Gould to Moe, February 20, 1936, Gould Guggenheim Files.

37. Millen Brand, April 4 and April 9, 1935, Journals, 1919–1943, Brand Papers, Box 76.

38. "Writer Honors 7,300,000th Word by Party," *New York Herald Tribune*, March 2, 1936. Gould told Pound, "I was fired for a while because I got too much publicity." Gould to Pound, May 30, 1938, Pound Papers, Box 19, Folder 861.

39. "800,000-Word History Book Unlimbers Its Author for More," *New York Herald Tribune*, April 10, 1937.

40. Savage to Arthur Schomburg, January 1935, quoted in Finkelstein, "Augusta Savage," 29–30.

41. Edgar T. Bouzeau, "Augusta Savage Is Commissioned by World's Fair," *Pittsburgh Courier*, December 18, 1937. For more on the commission, see the materials in the Rosenwald Archives, Box 127, Folder 7.

42. "Negroes: Their Artists Are Gaining in Skill and Recognition," *Life*, October 3, 1938, 55.

43. Bearden and Henderson, *History of African-American Artists*, 177. They speculate that the commission itself may have been a way for her to be removed.

44. "The best judgment of everybody in a position to know was that Mr. Gould's work was not essential." Henry G. Alsberg to Cummings, March 7, 1939, Cummings Papers, Additional II, Folder 15.

45. He says that here: E. L. Hendel and M. S. Singer, "Joe Gould '11, Poet, Dilettante, Bum, and Bohemian, Last of a Disappearing Species," *Harvard Crimson*, March 16, 1945. And also earlier: "I am, as you know, a very cosmopolychromatic person. Whatever form the thing takes will be colorful and good copy." Gould to Pound, December 22, 1932, Pound Papers, Box 19, Folder 861.

CHAPTER 10

1. "Artists Get New Inspiration from Augusta Savage Who Opens Gallery to Sell Their Work to the Public," *Chicago Defender*, June 10, 1939.

2. Savage describes some of the work of her studio in a letter to Edwin R. Embree, March 4, 1936, Rosenwald Archives, Box 127, Folder 7. On the Uptown Art Laboratory, see Savage to Embree, no date, same folder. And for a discussion of the Uptown Art Laboratory in the context of similar efforts, and of the WPA itself, see Erin Park Cohn, "Art Fronts: Visual Culture and Race Politics in the Mid-Twentieth-Century United States" (Ph.D. diss., University of Pennsylvania, 2010), chapter 2.

3. Savage to Thomas Elsa Jones, January 10, 1939 or 1940, Thomas Elsa Jones Collection, Fisk Library, Box 8, Folder 6.

4. Romare Bearden and Harry Henderson, *A History of African-American Artists: From 1792 to the Present* (New York: Pantheon, 1993), 177.

5. He did not see Gould during this visit. Gould later said, after Pound's arrest for treason, that he hadn't seen Pound then because he was out of political sympathy with him. Gould to Williams, February 8, 1946, Williams Papers, Box 7, Folder 243.

6. Pound to Cummings, 1933, *Pound/Cummings*, 4.

7. Cummings to Pound, May 1940, *Pound/Cummings*, 149.

8. William Saroyan, "How I Met Joe Gould," *Don Freeman's Newsstand* 1 (1941): 25, 27. And: "William Saroyan has adopted a 75-year-old Greenwich Villager yclept Joe Gould. The 'baby' has been penning a tome called 'The History of My Times from All Sources' for the past 20 years." Dorothy Kilgallen, "The Voice of Broadway," *Trenton Evening Times*, March 27, 1941.

9. Pound, "England," Broadcast #16, March 15, 1942, in *"Ezra Pound Speaking": Radio Speeches of World War II*, ed. Leonard W. Doob (Westport, CT: Greenwood Press, 1978), 59.

10. Mitchell, in his notes, said that his first interview with Gould was on June 10, 1942, Mitchell Papers, Box 9.1.

11. Cummings to Loren and Lloyd Frankenberg, July 2, 1942, Cummings Letters, Box 1.

12. Gould to Williams, October 1942, Williams Papers, Box 7, Folder 243.

13. Gould to Mumford, October 1942, Mumford Papers, Box 23, Folder 1906.

14. Mitchell, "Joe Gould's Secret."

15. Gould to Mumford, January 1943, Mumford Papers, Box 23, Folder 1906.

16. He didn't find out what happened next until May 8, when he finally got out of the hospital and got his

diary back. He wrote, "I looked in on Cummings. He said that Rex Hunter had seen me bleeding, unconscious and drunk at 23 St. An ambulance took me to Saint Vincent where I was treated for concussion of the skull. I apparently was released from there before Bellevue." Diary entries for January 13, 1943, and May 8, 1943, Gould Diaries. Hunter lived at Patchin Place. See Cummings to Qualey, January 16, 1947, Cummings and Qualey Papers, Box 1, Folder 19.

17. Cummings to Qualey, November 30, 1942, Cummings and Qualey Papers, Box 1, Folder 15. The reference is to Slater Brown's 1942 book *The Burning Wheel*, published by Bobbs-Merrill.

18. Brown to Mitchell, April 8, 1943, Mitchell Papers, Box 9.1.

19. Cummings to Qualey, March 13, 1943, Cummings and Qualey Papers, Box 1, Folder 15.

20. Brown to Mitchell, April 3, 1943, Mitchell Papers, Box 9.1. An alarming portrait of Wards Island at the time is Albert Deutsch, *The Shame of the States* (New York: Harcourt, Brace & Co., 1948), chapter 6, "New York's Isle of Despair." On Bellevue, see chapter 11, "Bellevue 'Psycho'—Famous and Forlorn."

21. Gould to Mitchell, April 3, 1943, Mitchell Papers, Box 9.1.

22. Gould to Mitchell, May 14, 1943, Mitchell Papers, Box 9.1. The publication of "Professor Sea Gull" did lead to the publication of a book by Gould, a chapbook of six very short poems: Joseph F. Gould, *VI* (Jacksonville-on-the-St-Johns, FL: Privately printed for John S. Mayfield, 1943).

23. Mitchell's notes on Gould, April 3, 1943, Mitchell Papers, Box 9.1.

24. Ibid. The category was far more capacious then. Alfred Margulies, email to the author, June 1, 2015. And see Elizabeth Lunbeck, *The Psychiatric Persua-*

sion: Knowledge, Gender and Power in Modern America (Princeton, NJ: Princeton University Press, 1994), 65–69.

25. Mitchell's notes on Gould, April 3, 1943; Brown to Mitchell, April 3, 1943; Gould to Mitchell, August 1, 1943, Mitchell Papers, Box 9.1.

26. Cummings to Qualey, January 4, 1944, Cummings and Qualey Papers, Box 1, Folder 16.

27. Gould to Cummings, July 1943: "Joe Mitchell's profile was reprinted in his book on McSorleys. (This is a place you and Nagel might remember. I don't. I never left there conscious.) This book is to be played up in the next issue of Time, and they took in my photo for the review. This should not hurt me none." Cummings Papers, Folder 490.

28. Diary entry for July 1, 1943, Gould Diaries.

29. Diary entry for July 30, 1943, Gould Diaries. And see also Gould to Cummings, August 23, 1943, Cummings Papers, Folder 490.

30. It was during this period that Gould sold Mitchell the dramatic rights to the story of his life. On *New Yorker* stationery, dated September 3, 1943, he wrote: "I, Joe Gould, for value received, give Mr. Joseph Mitchell permission to use or allow others to use creatively the material in his book 'McSorley's Wonderful Saloon,' in any stage or musical production." Mitchell Papers, Box 9.1.

31. Gould (c/o Slater Brown) to Mitchell, October 27, 1943, Mitchell Papers, Box 9.1.

32. Slater Brown interview, April 1960, Mitchell Papers, Box 9.1.

33. Slater Brown, "Page 3,769,300, Oral History of Our Time," one-page typescript, Cummings Papers, Folder 110.

34. Gould to Mumford, July 12, 1944, Mumford Papers, Box 23, Folder 1906.

35. Diary entry for March 4, 1945, Gould Diaries.

36. Diary entry for March 1, 1945, Gould Diaries.
37. E. L. Hendel and M. S. Singer, "Joe Gould '11, Poet, Dilettante, Bum, and Bohemian, Last of a Disappearing Species," *Harvard Crimson*, March 16, 1945. Gould asked for a retraction. "I met one of the Crimson boys there. He said that they had printed a partial ~~copy~~ retraction of their story." Diary entry for June 12, 1945, Gould Diaries.
38. Rev. Herb Gibney to Clyde Hart, October 13, 1992:

> Eventually Communist agents tried to use Augusta to influence young blacks with their political philosophy. When she refused, her life was threatened so she closed her studio and fled to the West. There she contracted Rocky Mountain Spotted Tick Fever and almost died. After her recovery she came back to the East, settled in Saugerties in the renovated hen house, and began to eke out a living raising chickens and selling their eggs. Eventually through a family in our church I was able to get her a job that gave her a sufficient income and thus permitted the continuance of her sculpturing.

This letter is in the possession of Karlyn Knaust Elia.
39. Millen Brand, Diary entry for February 26, 1942, Journals, 1919–1946, Brand Papers, Box 76.
40. In April and June 1941, Savage was questioned by the FBI in New York. She said she believed Gwendolyn Bennett to be "a Communist sympathizer" and recounted conversations the two women had had together while driving to and from the National Negro Congress in Philadelphia in 1937. (In 1939, Bennett replaced Savage at the Harlem Community Arts Center, and Savage believed, correctly, that she was not allowed to have the job back because

she herself wasn't a Communist.) Frances Pollock, who knew both women, encouraged the FBI to dismiss anything Savage might have said about Bennett on the ground that Savage was known to get "emotional" about Communism. But Savage's accusation, along with those of many other informants, proved damning; Bennett was fired. Gwendolyn Bennett File, Federal Works Agency, Work Projects Administration, Division of Investigation, June 19, 1941, case no. 5-NY-3717, especially pp. 6–8, 14. My great thanks to Patricia Hills for providing me with the FBI's account of Savage's testimony. Bennett's own FBI file and the files of many other Harlem Renaissance figures are available at the FBEyes Digital Archive, http://digital.wustl.edu/fbeyes/. For more on Bennett's files, see William Maxwell, *F.B. Eyes: How J. Edgar Hoover's Ghostreaders Framed African American Literature* (Princeton, NJ: Princeton University Press, 2015), 88–89.

41. Interviews with Karlyn Knaust Elia, Richard Duncan, John Finger, and Adrienne Nieffer, October 25, 2015. Heartfelt thanks to everyone in Saugerties who spoke with me.

CHAPTER 11

1. "Ye FBI has just sent us a pleasant Finn (whose name—according to him—is pronounced 'Illiterate') to explore Ezra Pound's right to anything, including death, for treason." Cummings to Qualey, February 15, 1943, Cummings and Qualey Papers, Box 1, Folder 15.

2. Gould to Macdonald, January 9, 1945: "Could you possibly use my article on Why Princeton Should Be Abolished?" Macdonald Papers, Box 19, Folder 479. Macdonald had published a piece by Gould in *Poli-*

tics in 1944: Joe Gould, "What to Do with Europe," *Politics*, May 1944, 111. It was sandwiched between "The Only Real Moral People . . ." by Irving Kristol and "The World of Moloch" by Daniel Bell. The contributors' page (128) lists him this way: "JOE GOULD is the author of an 'Oral History,' compiled exclusively from personal hearsay, which is as yet unpublished. He lives in New York City mostly, and also in Connecticut and on the Cape. His article and picture are reprinted, with permission, from *Don Freeman's Newsstand*."

3. Gould to Williams from Maison Gerard, February 8, 1946, Williams Papers, Box 7, Folder 243.

4. Diary entries, February 22, 24, 25, and 29, 1944, Gould Diaries.

5. Diary entry, March 4, 1944, Gould Diaries.

6. Diary entry, March 21, 1944, Gould Diaries.

7. Gould to Mitchell, April 20, 1944, Mitchell Papers, Box 9.1.

8. Diary entry, April 13, 1944, Gould Diaries.

9. Diary entry, April 28, 1944, Gould Diaries.

10. Rothschild to Gould, May 6, 1944, Mitchell Papers, Box 9.1.

11. Diary entry for May 11, 1943, Gould Diaries.

12. Diary entry for March 21, 1945, Gould Diaries. I unfortunately can't make out the name of the person he talked to at the Waldorf.

13. On the 1940s triumph of psychoanalysis in the United States, see Edward Shorter, *A History of Psychiatry: From the Era of the Asylum to the Age of Prozac* (New York: John Wiley & Sons, 1997), chapter 5, especially 170–81.

14. On that friendship and others, see Gardiner Reminiscences, 180–81, 260.

15. Ibid., 230.

16. My biography of Gardiner is reconstructed from her 422-page oral history interview, Gardiner

Reminiscences; her memoir, Muriel Gardiner, *Code Name "Mary": Memoirs of an American Woman in the Austrian Underground* (New Haven, CT: Yale University Press, 1983); a biography, Sheila Isenberg, *Muriel's War: An American Heiress in the Nazi Resistance* (New York: Palgrave Macmillan, 2010); and Muriel Gardiner, "Meetings with the Wolf-Man, 1938–1949," in *The Wolf-Man and Sigmund Freud*. Invaluable short summaries of her life are Samuel A. Guttman, "Muriel M. Gardiner, M.D. (1901–85)," *Psychoanalytic Study of the Child* 40 (1985): 1–7; and Fred B. Rogers, "Dr. Muriel M. Gardiner: Psychiatrist and Philanthropist," *New Jersey Medicine* 86 (March 1989): 193–95. See also Janet Malcolm, *In the Freud Archives* (New York: Alfred A. Knopf, 1984).

17. Mitchell, interview with Gardiner, Princeton, June 30, 1959, Mitchell Papers, Box 10.1.

18. Gardiner Reminiscences, 190.

19. Mitchell, interview with Erika Feist, June 1959, Mitchell Papers, Box 9.1.

20. It's also possible that Gardiner's brother, who was born in 1891, knew Gould at Harvard. On her brother attending Harvard, see Gardiner Reminiscences, 7.

21. Gardiner Reminiscences, 43–45.

22. "Dr. Gardiner has always made available a very considerable portion of her annual income to literally hundreds of people and a large number of organizations." Guttman, "Muriel M. Gardiner." Gardiner began giving Neel $6,000 a year in 1964. Ann Harvey [Gardiner's granddaughter], email to the author, June 19, 2015.

23. Gardiner Reminiscences, 257.

24. Mitchell, interview with Gardiner, Princeton, June 30, 1959, Mitchell Papers, Box 10.1. Rothschild told Mitchell that "she helped G simply because people she liked told her it was a good thing to do."

Mitchell's interview with Rothschild, June 18, 1959, Mitchell Papers, Box 9.1.

25. Gardiner, *The Wolf-Man and Sigmund Freud*, 315.

26. This begins in the diaries on May 22, 1945, and continues. It's also the subject of all of Gould's letters from this point on, for months. See, for example, Gould to James Laughlin, June 2, 1945, New Directions Records, Folder 655.

27. Gould to Macdonald from the Maison Gerard, June 4, 1945, Macdonald Papers, Box 19, Folder 479. Also, from Gould's diary, May 29, 1945: "I saw Dwight MacDonald. I explained about Pound. He gave me a dollar and some back issues." Gould Diaries.

28. Gould to James Laughlin, June 19, 1945, New Directions Records, Folder 655.

29. Gould to Cowley, June 4, 1945, Cowley Papers, Box 106, Folder 5000. And, "Some amateur Guggenheim is subsidizing me." Gould to Mitchell, May 1945, Mitchell Papers, Box 9.1.

30. Gould to Williams, October 13, 1946, Williams Papers, Box 7, Folder 243.

31. Pound to Cummings, November 20, 1946, *Pound/Cummings*, 201.

32. Cummings to Qualey, October 16, 1946, Cummings and Qualey Papers, Box 1, Folder 18.

33. Cummings to Pound, May 1948, *Pound/Cummings*, 231.

34. Mitchell, interview with Gardiner, Princeton, June 30, 1959, Mitchell Papers, Box 10.1.

35. Erika Feist, interview, June 1959, Mitchell Papers, Box 9.1.

36. Vivian Marquie, interview, May 1959, Mitchell Papers, Box 9.1.

37. John Rothschild to Muriel Gardiner, October 10, 1947, Mitchell Papers, Box 9.1.

38. Reminiscences of Allan Nevins, 1963, Columbia Oral History Project, 169–70, 232, 235–42.

39. Louis Starr, "Oral History," in *Oral History: An Interdisciplinary Anthology*, ed. David K. Dunaway and Willa K. Baum (Walnut Creek, CA: AltaMira Press, 1996), 43–44.

40. Gould to Sarton, 1931, George Sarton Additional Papers, MS Am 1803, Folder 655, Houghton Library, Harvard University. The letter to Sarton is the only one of these I've found in an archive, but Gould invariably sent identical letters to multiple recipients asking for money and support, as he did here. I find it difficult to believe he didn't send a very similar letter to Nevins. The language Gould used in his letter to Sarton is the same as he had been using in describing the Oral History for several years; it was part of what was essentially a letter that he must have sent out en masse. On Nevins (and his great man theory of history), see Gerald L. Fetner, *Immersed in Great Affairs: Allan Nevins and the Heroic Age of American History* (Albany: State University of New York Press, 2004).

41. Nevins issued his first public call in 1938, in *The Gateway to History:* "We have agencies aplenty to seek out the papers of men long dead. But we have only the most scattered and haphazard agencies for obtaining a little of the immense mass of information about the more recent American past—the past of the last half century—which might come fresh and direct from men once prominent in politics, in business, in the professions, and in other fields; information that every obituary column shows to be perishing." Nevins is quoted in Starr, "Oral History," 43–44. The project's focus on great men in its early decades is well illustrated by the collections, and their use in books described at its twentieth anniversary, in Columbia University Oral History Research Office, *Oral History: The First Twenty Years* (New York: Columbia University, 1968). At just the

moment of that anniversary, though, the political movements of the 1960s, alongside the resurgence of social history, transformed the collections. A very good description of that change is Columbia University Oral History Research Office, *Oral History* (New York: Columbia University, 1992).

42. Reminiscences of Allan Nevins, 242.

43. Gould to Cummings, December 2, 1947, Cummings Papers, Folder 490.

44. Omar Pound to Marion Cummings, December 8, 1947 ("Thanks for a most enjoyable evening, and the onions! . . . ps. met joe gould before i left"), Cummings Additional Papers II; Pound to Cummings, December 8, 1947; Cummings to Pound, December 1947, *Pound/Cummings*, 226.

CHAPTER 12

1. Pilgrim State Hospital opened in 1931 with two thousand patients. Its one hundred buildings covered two thousand acres. Alfred Eistenstaedt photographed Pilgrim for *Time* in 1938. By 1950 it had eleven thousand patients. Jack Pressman, *Last Resort: Psychosurgery and the Limits of Medicine* (New York: Cambridge University Press, 1998), 173–76. Pressman writes, "Pilgrim's prefrontal lobotomy program had become its clinical showpiece" (174).

2. I requested Gould's medical records from what is now the Pilgrim Psychiatric Center on April 15, 2015; my request was denied (Deborah Strube, Chairperson, Medical Records Access Review Committee, Pilgrim Psychiatric Center, to the author, April 17, 2015). I appealed that decision (author to Strube, April 29 and 30, 2015), and Pilgrim again declined my request (Strube, email to the author, May 15, 2015).

3. Chances are very good that Gould was treated with electroshock, and lobotomized, and, when that didn't work, drugged into a stupor that ended only with his death. In some ways drug therapies were a response to the successful treatment of general paresis of the insane with the blood of malarial victims. Early, pre-1950 twentieth-century drug therapies included sedatives and barbiturates. On the early drug regimes, see Edward Shorter, *A History of Psychiatry: From the Era of the Asylum to the Age of Prozac* (New York: John Wiley & Sons, 1997), 196–207; on electroshock, 218–24; on lobotomy, 225–29. Shorter quotes Gerard Grob: "By 1951, no fewer than 18,608 individuals had undergone psychosurgery since its introduction in 1936." In 1949 alone, more than five thousand lobotomies were conducted in U.S. hospitals (228). The new generation of antipsychotic drugs did not debut until 1954 (228). Allen Ginsberg's mother, Naomi, was lobotomized at Pilgrim State in 1949, with Ginsberg's consent; he was twenty-one. Naomi Ginsberg never left Pilgrim State and died there in 1956. Gould and Naomi Ginsberg overlapped at Pilgrim; they had also known one another much earlier in life, in the 1920s, and she claimed to have had an affair with Gould's archnemesis, Max Bodenheim. Barry Miles, *Allen Ginsberg: Beat Poet* (1989; London: Virgin Books, 2010), 8.

4. Morton M. Hunt, "Pilgrim's Progress, Part I," *New Yorker*, September 30, 1961, and Hunt, "Pilgrim's Progress, Part II," *New Yorker*, October 7, 1961. An enlargement of Hunt's two essays was printed as a book: Morton M. Hunt, *Mental Hospital* (New York: Pyramid Books, 1962), with a foreword by Robert H. Felix, M.D., director of the National Institute of Mental Health. The book, like the articles, is a chronicle and celebration of the triumph of the new psychiatric regime. The back cover copy of

the paperback reads, "The snake-pit is becoming non-existent!" (*The Snake Pit* was the title of a 1948 film about an insane asylum; the Oscar-nominated script was written by Millen Brand.) For a more recent vantage on Pilgrim, see a memoir by the daughter of a former patient: Jacqueline Walker, *Pilgrim State* (London: Sceptre, 2008). Walker's mother, Dorothy Walker, was committed to Pilgrim State in 1949.

5. Harry J. Worthing, M.D., "A Report on Electric Shock Treatment at Pilgrim State Hospital," *Psychiatric Quarterly* 15 (1941): 306–9. And see Worthing et al., "The Organization and Administration of a State Hospital Insulin-Metrazol-Electric Shock Therapy Unit," *American Journal of Psychiatry* 99 (1943): 692–97.

6. Harry J. Worthing, M.D., Henry Brill, M.D., and Henry Widgerson, M.D., "350 Cases of Prefrontal Lobotomy," *Psychiatric Quarterly* 23 (1949): 617–56. And see Henry Brill, "The Place of Neurosurgery in the Treatment Program of a Department of Mental Hygiene," *New York State Journal of Medicine* 52 (October 15, 1952): 2503–7. Pressman argues that lobotomy was at the center, not the fringe, of medical practice, and that it emerged out of earlier practices. He also takes issue with popular accounts that demonize lobotomy, which is useful, although his efforts to rehabilitate the practitioners who conducted, for instance, more than five thousand lobotomies in 1949 alone is unpersuasive. See Pressman, *Last Resort*, 172–77.

7. Worthing et al., "350 Cases," 626–27.

8. Ibid., 632.

9. Ibid., 645.

10. "Greatest expansion occurred in the surgical division. A total of 265 major operations were performed, including 205 prefrontal lobotomies. This compares with the figures of 112 for the previous

year of which 33 were lobotomies." And "the central shock therapy unit also provided special care to 124 patients (94 female and 30 male) following prefrontal lobotomy." Pilgrim State Hospital, *Annual Report* (New York, 1948), 12–15.

11. Pressman, *Last Resort*, 180.

12. See Worthing et al., "350 Cases," 626. In Gould's case, either the hospital believed he had no family, or else they received consent from Chassan, Gould's niece. Chassan was in agony about her uncle when Mitchell interviewed her after Gould's death. And when "Joe Gould's Secret" came out, Mitchell wrote to Chassan that he had decided not to mention anything she had told him; these were details concerning the family's history of mental illness and psychiatric treatment (including Chassan's own). Brill explained that patients suffering from dementia praecox (schizophrenia) tended not to respond well to shock, which is why they were the patients most likely to be lobotomized. Brill, "The Place of Neurosurgery," 2503–4. Brill may have been involved in Gould's lobotomy, as well as in that of Ginsberg's mother. In October 1952 he reported, "The author's experience with lobotomy was gained . . . when he worked with a series of 600 cases of lobotomy done at Pilgrim State Hospital, New York, between the years 1945 and 1950. (The number in this series now stands above 1,100.) Many of the patients had been known to him for periods of five years and longer; each was chosen for operation personally after discussion with the family and careful review of the record. Initiative was practically always taken by the hospital and in no case was a patient operated at the insistence of relatives when it seemed medically not indicated" (2505). The surgery itself was done by Henry Widgerson.

13. Worthing et al., "350 Cases," 654.

14. Gould to Williams, May 27, 1949, Williams Papers, Box 7, Folder 243. During that period, though, Cummings did see him. "I've been seeing a lot of Joe G lately," Cummings wrote to Pound in May 1948, *Pound/Cummings*, 231. This is explained, though, if Cummings visited Gould at that time.

15. Postcard stamped February 1950, sent to Macdonald by the Department of Hospitals, Bellevue Hospital. On one side are visiting hours and policies; on the other, a form filled out "Dear Sir or Madam: [handwritten 'Joseph Gould'] has been admitted to Bellevue Hospital and has given your name as that of the nearest friend or relative." Macdonald Papers, Box 19, Folder 479. "I was on Joe's calling list in the later years; toward the end, I arranged with Dorothy Day to have him taken into a Catholic Worker of hospitality up the Hudson, he stayed there a while (a month maybe) but left—he'd become bored and the inhabitants also, with him—he needed a constant turnover audience, as you note, for his sake, and theirs." Macdonald to Mitchell, on *New Yorker* stationery, October 15, 1964, Mitchell Papers, Box 10.1.

16. Chassan saw him once more, the next year: It was through Dorothy Day that Colleen Chassan "had her last contact with Joe Gould in 1952." Mary L. Holman, Work Summary, October 23, 1957, Mitchell Papers, Box 9.1.

17. Morris Werner sent Worthing five dollars, to pay for some cigarettes for Gould, but, Werner said, "I . . . expected and of course got no letter, as by that time he was too far gone." Werner to Mitchell, September 25, 1964, Mitchell Papers, Box 10.1.

18. Hunt, "Pilgrim's Progress, Part II." In "Pilgrim's Progress, Part I," Hunt's history of the rise of tranquilizers and their place in the history of psychiatric hospitalization is largely a transcription of a his-

tory given to him by Worthing's successor, Henry
Brill.

19. Hunt, "Pilgrim's Progress, Part I." And see Hunt,
    Mental Hospital, 42–44.

20. Notes about a phone call with Ed Gottlieb, June 20,
    1957, Mitchell Papers, Box 9.1.

21. Gould to Pound, 1928, Pound Papers, Box 19,
    Folder 861.

22. Harry Worthing, M.D., to Slater Brown, August 19,
    1957, by telegram. Mitchell Papers, Box 9.1.

23. Michael Cipollino, Chief Clerk, Suffolk County
    Surrogates' Court, to the author, May 12, 2015.

24. Mitchell, "Joe Gould's Secret."

25. Mitchell, notes from August 21, 1957, Mitchell
    Papers, Box 9.1.

26. Ibid.

27. Mitchell, notes from August 22, 1957, Mitchell
    Papers, Box 9.1.

28. "Joe Gould Saved from Potter's Field," *Washington
    Post*, August 22, 1957. On the alleged Joe Gould
    scholarship at NYU, see Charles Hutchinson and
    Peter Miller, "Joe Gould's Secret History," *Village
    Voice*, April 4, 2000.

29. *Time*, September 2, 1957. And also "Joe Gould Dead;
    'Last Bohemian,'" *New York Times*, August 20, 1957.
    (The *Time* obituary is cribbed from the *Times*.)

30. Dan Balaban, "Last Rites for a Bohemian," *Village
    Voice*, August 28, 1957.

31. Chris Cominel to Cummings, August 20, 1957, Cum-
    mings Papers, Folder 251.

32. Mitchell's notes about interviewing Margules,
    September and October 1957, Mitchell Papers,
    Box 9.1.

33. That it was Chassan who hired Holman is revealed in
    Holman to Mitchell, September 25, 1964, Mitchell
    Papers, Box 9.1. And see Holman to Mitchell, Sep-
    tember 30, 1957; Holman to Mitchell, October 23,

1957; telephone call with Holman, October 9, 1957; telephone call with Holman, May 21, 1959, Mitchell Papers, Box 9.1.

34. Holman, "Work Summary," October 23, 1957, Mitchell Papers, Box 9.1.

35. See Mitchell's interviews with Woodman, November 7, 1957, and with Nalbud, June 23, 1958, and May 20, 1959, Mitchell Papers, Box 9.1.

36. Nalbud, May 20, 1959, interview, Mitchell Papers, Box 9.1.

37. Nalbud, letter to the editor, Harvard Crimson, April 30, 1958, Nathan Pusey Papers, Harvard University Archives.

38. This produced a long chain of letters in the Pusey Papers, most of them from April and May 1958.

39. Nalbud, June 23, 1958, interview, Mitchell Papers, Box 9.1. And see the flyer itself.

40. James Nalbud, mass-mailed postcard, April 17, 1959, Mitchell Papers, Box 9.1.

41. Pound to Cummings, April 14, 1958, Pound/Cummings, 399.

42. Gould, "Why I Write."

43. Romare Bearden and Harry Henderson, A History of African-American Art: From 1792 to the Present (New York: Pantheon, 1993), 180.

44. Obituaries include Chester Hampton, "Augusta Savage Dies," Baltimore Afro-American, April 7, 1962.

45. On Savage's fate, see the Hugh Samson letters, Smithsonian Archives of American Art, and Theresa Leininger-Miller, New Negro Artists in Paris: African American Painters and Sculptors in the City of Light, 1922–1934 (New Brunswick, NJ: Rutgers University Press, 2001), 162. "Memories of Augusta Savage in Saugerties," Auction Finds, October 14, 2010. Karlyn Knaust Elia, emails to the author, October 7, 10, and 22, 2015.

46. Richard A. Hitchcock to Mitchell, November 11,

1965, Mitchell Papers, Box 9.1. Hitchcock's is a long and detailed letter. Hitchcock is all over Gould's diary.

47. Jane Magill, New York, to Mitchell, October 22, 1964, Mitchell Papers, Box 10.1.

Index

Page numbers beginning with 161 refer to endnotes.

A NOTE ABOUT THE AUTHOR

Jill Lepore is the David Woods Kemper '41 Professor of American History at Harvard University and a staff writer at *The New Yorker.* Her books include *The Secret History of Wonder Woman*, a *New York Times* best seller, and *Book of Ages*, a finalist for the National Book Award. She lives in Cambridge, Massachusetts.

A NOTE ON THE TYPE

This book was set in Janson, a typeface named for the Dutchman Anton Janson, but actually the work of Nicholas Kis (1650–1702), a Hungarian, who most probably learned his trade from the master Dutch typefounder Dirk Voskens. The type is an example of the Dutch types that prevailed in England up to the time of William Caslon (1692–1766).

Typeset by Scribe,
Philadelphia, Pennsylvania

Printed and bound by RR Donnelley,
Harrisonburg, Virginia

Designed by Maggie Hinders